A SHORT HISTORY OF BELGIUM

THE UNIVERSITY OF CHICAGO PRESS
CHICAGO, ILLINOIS

Agents

THE BAKER & TAYLOR COMPANY
NEW YORK

THE CUNNINGHAM, CURTISS & WELCH COMPANY
LOS ANGELES

THE CAMBRIDGE UNIVERSITY PRESS
LONDON AND EDINBURGH

THE MARUZEN-KABUSHIKI-KAISHA
TOKYO, OSAKA, KYOTO

THE MISSION BOOK COMPANY
SHANGHAI

KARL W. HIERSEMANN
LEIPZIG

A SHORT HISTORY
OF BELGIUM

BY

LÉON VAN DER ESSEN, PH.D., LL.D.

Professor of History in the University of Louvain
Member of the Royal Academy of Archaeology
of Belgium

THE UNIVERSITY OF CHICAGO PRESS
CHICAGO, ILLINOIS

Composed and Printed By
The University of Chicago Press
Chicago, Illinois, U.S.A.

TO

ALBERT I

KING OF THE BELGIANS

THE KNIGHT WITHOUT FEAR AND WITHOUT REPROACH

CONTENTS

INTRODUCTION

The "New York Times Review of Books" of June 20, 1915, called attention to the comparative scarcity of books on Belgium among the literary productions resulting from the war, and continued: "Why Belgium finds so scant a space in the war bibliographies is a question difficult to answer. Certainly, no country has aroused the popular sympathy and enthusiasm of the world to a like degree with this little kingdom, occupying a geographical area of about one-fourth the state of Pennsylvania, yet performing deeds of valour and enduring martyrdoms that place it beyond all comparison in greatness. If the war has a hero it is Belgium: hence, one argues, that country should fill a prominent instead of a slight section in the literature of the great conflict."

This idea, doubtless, it was that induced the University of Chicago Press to propose that I write and publish under its auspices a *Short History of Belgium*, with material drawn from the course of lectures I gave on the history of Belgium at the University of Chicago during the Winter Quarter of 1915.

This *Short History of Belgium*, of course, is not a "war book" and cannot be placed among those books classed as war literature. The circumstances of its being written have some connection, of course, with the great war, but it hardly needs to be said that this history is objective and tries simply to give an account of the past history of the Belgian people, leaving entirely out of consideration their present deeds and sufferings. By consulting that history

1

the reader will, however, be able to understand much more clearly than he did before why the Belgian nation of today took the stand it has taken in the great war and preferred honor in place of dishonor, and struggle for freedom in place of ease. The fight of the Flemish communes against the King of France in the fourteenth century, the great struggle against Spain in the sixteenth century, the revolt against Austrian rule in the eighteenth century, and the revolution of 1830 are examples and inspiration for the Belgians of today.

There has been much discussion about the time at which Belgian history should be said to begin. Belgium, as an entirely autonomous, independent kingdom, has existed only since 1830. But the Belgium of 1830 was, in a certain way, a creation of European diplomacy and the result of centuries of struggle for personal and political freedom. Belgium, as a country, and the Belgians, as a people, existed long before. Since the time of Caesar (57 B.C.), history tells us of the Belgians, "the bravest of all the people of Gaul," and, although the Germanic invasions of the fourth and fifth centuries have added a new ethnical element to the old Belgian stock, it is from the time of the Roman conqueror that the history of the Belgian people really begins. As for Belgium as a united political body, one must go back to the fifteenth century, when the dukes of Burgundy succeeded in unifying all the Belgian duchies and counties under one dynasty. Before that time, Belgium had practically consisted of two very distinct parts, Lotharingia in the east, Flanders in the west, separated by the river Scheldt. Lotharingia was, politically speaking, a part of the mediaeval German empire; Flanders was in subjugation to the kingdom of France. Each succeeded

—Lotharingia first, then Flanders—in evading the political domination of Germany and France, respectively, and drew closer and closer together during the last centuries of the Middle Ages. That work of union was achieved by the Burgundian dukes, who inherited from the local Lotharingian and Flemish dynasties, in the fifteenth century.

But in the Middle Ages not only did the increasing tendency of union between Lotharingia and Flanders exist, but there was also a strong factor of national union, the common civilization, the common culture, of Lotharingia and Flanders. The inhabitants of the different duchies and counties were united by the same religion, the same artistic and economic aims, the same political institutions, although there were, of course, some local differences of minor importance. Since early in the Middle Ages the Belgian people had possessed a distinctive though mutually common civilization, and the local differences which existed and which were more or less well defined at the outset disappeared gradually as the different parts of the country drew closer together politically.

The history of Belgium and the Belgian people does not begin to date merely from 1830, not even from the fifteenth century. It dates in fact from the time when, during the fifth century, Gallo-Romans and Germanic invaders intermingled and laid the basis of that ethnical and linguistic duality that has been for many centuries the characteristic of the Belgian populace and has impressed its mark on the whole course of Belgian history.

The real unity of the history of Belgium in antemodern times has been brought into notice by one of Belgium's leading historians, Henri Pirenne, professor in the University of Ghent, in his admirable work, *Histoire de Belgique*. Before the publication of this work, few scholars understood how to treat the history of Belgium during the Middle Ages. Having in mind only the political aspect of that history, they were lost in the particular history of the various duchies and counties; they saw scarcely any link between the facts of these different historical sections, and they forgot entirely to take account of the unifying factor—the common culture and civilization.

Since historians have had their attention called to that unifying factor, the history of Belgium has been looked upon in a different manner. It is in the light of that method that I shall try to explain the course of the historical development of the country.

The national culture of Belgium is a synthesis, if I may so call it, where one finds the genius of two races—the Romance and the Germanic—mingled, yet modified by the imprint of the distinctively Belgian. It is in that very receptivity—the fact that it has absorbed and unified the best elements of Latin and Teutonic civilization—that the originality of the Belgian national culture resides.

These distinctive marks of national culture, denoting the unity of a people, and serving, both in the Middle Ages and today, to distinguish the Belgian nation from the other nations of Europe, may be described as a common desire for independence and freedom, a jealous regard for those popular rights which serve as a guaranty of the continuance of independence and freedom, and a deeply religious spirit. In the course of their history the Belgians have always cast off the yoke of those princes who, like Philip II, Joseph II, and William I of Holland, attacked their liberties and privileges, or who, like Joseph II and William I of Holland, tried to impose their own religious beliefs on them.

Those characteristics of the Belgian nation, as well as its common civilization, were born during the Middle Ages. For that reason I shall deal in a special manner with the different aspects of religious, artistic, literary, and economic life during that period. After the treatment of the political unity of the Belgian provinces achieved in the fifteenth century, more attention will be given to the political aspect of events, without, however, entirely neglecting the different forms of popular life and social activity.

The history of Belgium may be divided into the following periods: (1) the formative period, including the time of the Roman occupation, the invasion of the Franks, and the reign of Charles the Great and his immediate heirs (57 B.C. to 843 A.D.); (2) the period of feudalism; (3) the rise of the communes (eleventh to fourteenth century); (4) the political centralization of the dukes of Burgundy (fifteenth century); (5) the Spanish rule (sixteenth to seventeenth century); (6) the Austrian rule (eighteenth century); (7) the French régime (1792–1815); (8) the Dutch rule and the revolution of 1830; (9) the period of national independence.

During all these periods of history the names "Belgium" and "Belgians" have not been uniformly those by which the country and its people have been designated. The name "Belgae," of Celtic origin, was given in Caesar's time to the confederation of Celtic tribes which occupied the territory of Belgium, when for the first time the Roman legions came in contact with them. The name Belgium,

"Belgica," disappeared with the Roman occupation and does not reappear until the sixteenth century. During the sixteenth century, and especially at the beginning of the seventeenth, the name "Belgium" is to be found in books, but seems not to have been used as a common designation. As a distinctive name for a race or people, the term "Belges" became generally used at the end of the eighteenth century, its adjectival form being then "belgique" (les provinces belgiques, "the Belgian provinces"). Between the end of the Roman occupation and the end of the eighteenth century the Belgians were successively known as "Franks," "Lotharingi," and "Flemings." Since the thirteenth century, the country itself has been called "Netherlands" (partes advallenses), when the name Lotharingia disappeared as a political term. The term "Burgundian provinces" was sometimes used in the fifteenth century, while the name "Flanders," "Fiandra," "Flandes," was mainly applied during the Spanish rule. During the Austrian rule, the name "Austrian Netherlands" was the prevailing designation.[1] The term "Netherlands" was applied, not only to the actual territory of Belgium, but to the countries which today correspond to the territories included in the kingdoms of Belgium and Holland. From the time of the Roman occupation until 1588 Belgium and Holland have, indeed, a somewhat common history. Since 1588, when the provinces of the north separated from the south as the United Provinces of the Netherlands, Belgium and Holland have existed as separate states, and have no longer a common history.

We shall not attempt to deal here with the history of the northern provinces from the early Middle Ages down

[1] See G. Kurth, Notre nom national.

to 1588, for that is the task of the historian of Holland, and although, politically speaking, the provinces of Belgium and Holland both shared the same vicissitudes until 1588, yet, as has been pointed out by Professor Colenbrander,[1] from the point of view of artistic, literary, and economic life, the national culture of the two was quite distinct.

On the other hand, included in this history is that of the principality of Liège. Liège was never a part of the Netherlands; until 1795 it was an ecclesiastical state with a separate entity, ruled by bishops, princes of the Holy Roman Empire. But Liège had a civilization, and especially institutions, common to those of the other Belgian provinces, and, geographically and historically speaking, it was really a part of Belgium.

Having thus indicated what is to be dealt with in this *Short History of Belgium*, it remains only to mention the bibliographical list appended at the close of the work, which includes the most important books on general Belgian history. A reference to these will facilitate a deeper study of the subject and will enable the student to enter more in detail into the history of the country.[2]

LÉON VAN DER ESSEN

[1] H. Colenbrander, *De Belgische Omwenteling*.

[2] I am much indebted for the drawing of the maps in the book to Mr. Isidore Versluys, librarian of the Historical Seminary in the University of Louvain.

CHAPTER I

THE PERIOD OF FORMATION

When, in 57 B.C., the Roman Republic, then in control of most of the Mediterranean countries, the south of Gaul included, determined to conquer also the rest of that country, Belgium was occupied by a people of Celtic origin, called the Belgians, "Belgae." They were a part of the larger group of the Gauls who possessed the country between the Pyrennees, the Alps, the Rhine, and the sea. The Belgians occupied, not only the actual territory of Belgium, but also a part of Northern France and of Rhenish Prussia. They formed a confederation of several tribes, among which the Nervians, dwelling in the provinces of Hainaut, Brabant, and Flanders, were the most important.

The Roman general, Julius Caesar, intrusted with the task of subduing the north of Gaul, attacked the Belgians in 57 B.C. The Roman army would have been routed by the Nervians in the first attack but for Caesar, who himself led the troops and saved the day. Notwithstanding a fierce guerrilla warfare that lasted four years, all the Belgian tribes were successively subdued and some of them exterminated. Their heroic resistance made Caesar say of them: "Among all the Gauls, the bravest are the Belgians."

Once subdued, Belgium accepted the Roman rule and remained loyal to the Empire. Civilization was rapidly introduced; great military roads were constructed through the Belgian forests and marshes, connecting the different towns, and along their course villages were built and farms developed. Tongres and Tournai became entirely Romanized cities, where splendid monuments were built; remains of these are still to be found today. Farms were laid out and country houses were erected according to Roman pattern, with such changes as were imposed by the rigors of the northern climate. The Belgians adopted Roman manners and customs and the Latin language: they became Gallo-Romans, and even the national gods were renamed with Roman names.

If Belgium shared the splendor and the civilization of the Roman Empire, it shared also the disastrous days of its decline. There came a time when the Empire, once so strong, but now growing weaker and weaker, was quite unable to resist the hordes of barbarians, which, coming from the dark forests of Germany, threatened the rich provinces of Gaul, and Italy itself, with invasion. From the third century on, Franks and Alamans devastated Gaul and left the wealthy territories covered with ruins. The emperors did not succeed in expelling the Franks from the country: those tribes of Teutonic race were allowed to remain in the northern parts of Belgium, Flanders and Campine,[1] and became soldiers of the Empire. They early became dissatisfied with the territory allotted to them and resumed their march southward, conquering the whole of Belgium. The year 406 witnessed a terrible catastrophe. The Teutons, driven out of their country by the invasion of the Huns, burst like a hurricane upon

---

[1] A wide expanse of sandy soil extends from east to west almost uninterruptedly across Belgium; the eastern section of this, covering the northeastern portions of the provinces of Antwerp and Limburg, is called the Campine. Cf. R. C. K. Ensor, *Belgium*, p. 24.

the unfortunate provinces of Belgium, burned and devastated everything on their march, destroyed Tongres and Tournai, and finally, swarming over the Alps and the Pyrennees, invaded both Italy and Spain. After their passage, Belgium was left undefended by the Roman legions, recalled to defend Italy itself, and the Franks of Flanders and Campine occupied the abandoned territory without difficulty.

The conquest by the Franks is an important event in Belgian history. Indeed, it is from the fifth century that the bilingualism and the ethnographical dualism of Belgium may be said to date. The Franks, composed of two tribes, the Salians and the Ripuarians, advanced from the north and the east into Belgium and occupied the country in such a way that the actual provinces of Flanders, Antwerp, Limburg, the larger part of Brabant, and Liège fell into their power. Farther south they did not enter Belgium: their march was stopped by a dense and extended forest which, in Southwestern and Central Belgium, constituted the continuation of the forests of the Ardennes. The forest in question was called Sylva Carbonaria, "Coal Wood," and covered the largest part of the actual province of Hainaut, the seat of the modern Belgian coal industry. Behind the curtain of that forest the oldest inhabitants of the country, the Gallo-Romans, remained free from oppression by the invaders and retained their Latin culture and civilization. So Belgium was separated by the Sylva Carbonaria into two quite distinct parts: the northern part, occupied by the Franks, with their Teutonic culture and civilization; the southern part, occupied by the Gallo-Romans. A line was thus drawn dividing the Belgian people, and an ethnical and linguistic duality, destined to remain for centuries one of the main characteristics of the country, was established. Indeed, the Walloons[1] of today are the descendants of the old Gallo-Romans from behind the limits of the Sylva Carbonaria, and the Flemings of Northern Belgium are the descendants of the Franks. This line drawn in the fifth century has undergone little change in the course of ages and, although the famous coal wood disappeared many centuries ago, the separation between Walloons and Flemings has remained more or less apparent down to the present. In this case the Sylva Carbonaria played a part like that of the Alps in the case of the Romanches and the Italians of the Tessino, and that of the hills of Wales and Cornwall in the case of the Britons of England.

The first king of the Franks known in history is Clodion, who conquered the countries of Tournai and Cambrai and established the seat of his realm in Tournai. It is in this town that his grave was discovered in 1653; the King was found buried, according to the customs of his people, together with his arms and royal ornaments; he was identified by the presence of a ring on which his likeness and his name were engraved.

It was from Tournai that the famous descendant of Clodion, King Clodovech, started his campaign of further conquest that gave him possession of Northern France and, after the war against the Burgundians and the Westgoths (506), the control of nearly the whole of their

[1] The term "Walloon" comes from *Wala*, "foreigner," the name that was given by the Teutonic invaders to the Gallo-Romans dwelling behind the Sylva Carbonaria. The name *Wala* is to be connected with the terms "Welsh," "Wales," apparently of the same origin and given to the Britons and their country by the Anglo-Saxon invaders.

country. From this time on, the Frankish kings established their capital at Paris. Belgium is no longer associated with the recollection of their glorious deeds.

Clodion and his successors, so far as we know by the general history of Europe, belonged to the so-called dynasty of the Merovingians. The kings of that dynasty, in the course of the seventh century, were weaklings, actually dominated by their powerful ministers, the mayors of the palace. One of these, Peppin, in 751, succeeded in becoming himself a king and was the founder of a new royal dynasty, the Carolingians.

The new dynasty was, geographically speaking, essentially a Belgian dynasty, for it had many possessions in Eastern Belgium and all its members had occupied influential offices at the court of the Austrasian kings, who, in the sixth and seventh centuries, ruled over that part of the country.

The most famous of the Carolingians is Charles the Great, who re-established the old Roman Empire (800) and who, by successful campaigns, succeeded in extending his domination over the territory lying between the river Elbe, the Bohemian mountains, and the Raab on the east, the sea on the west, the North Sea, and the Garigliano River in Italy and the Ebro River in Spain on the south.

The favorite residence of the great Emperor was at Aix, and this contributed largely to the development of Belgian trade and industry at the beginning of the ninth century. Politically abandoned by the Frankish kings when they moved to Paris, Belgium again became important in the time of Charles the Great as the most favorably located portion of the Frankish Empire.

Belgium is, indeed, for trade purposes, the natural meeting-ground of the West-European nations. Lying between England, France, Germany, and Holland, it has good water communications with each. Though not quite so near the English coast as a corner of France is, it has the great advantage of exactly fronting the mouth of the Thames. With France it is connected by the upper courses of the Lys, the Scheldt, the Sambre, and the Meuse, the last named being navigable by deep-draught vessels far into Lorraine. With Germany its connection is less direct, the outlet of the Rhine running of course through Holland.[1]

These geographical conditions played a large part in the development of Belgian trade in the time of Charles the Great. The presence of the imperial palace at Aix attracted a great deal of traffic: from every part of the empire merchants, soldiers, priests, in short all classes of people, came through Belgium in order to reach the residence of the Emperor, and their presence resulted in unparalleled prosperity in that part of the Carolingian empire. Charles the Great was not only a great soldier and legislator, but also a good Christian. During his reign the development of religious life in the different parts of the empire grew rapidly.

Something ought to be said concerning the introduction of the Christian religion into Belgium. The preaching of the gospel in Belgium goes back as far as the Roman occupation of the time of the Empire, but the religious organization of the church in the country dates from the middle of the fourth century. At that time we find in the city of Tongres the oldest historically known

[1] R. C. K. Ensor, *Belgium*, pp. 37–38.

bishop of Belgium, St. Servatius. The historical origin of the bishoprics of Arras, Tournai, Boulogne, Cambrai—all of them at that time in Belgian territory—remains a matter of conjecture. The baptism of King Clodovech in 496 made the development of the Christian religion easier, although the conversion of the King to the Catholic faith did not at all mean the conversion of the whole people. Large parts of Belgium, especially the eastern part, remained heathen until the eighth century, and the introduction of the Christian religion in these sections of the country is mainly the work of missionaries. These missionaries worked on their own initiative, without any such prearranged plan as, for instance, existed for the introduction of Catholicism into England. It was mainly by Irish and Anglo-Saxon missionaries that the gospel was made known, and the most famous of those heralds of the Catholic religion was the Anglo-Saxon missionary Willibrord. The work of the missionaries was completed by the bishops, who visited large portions of their very extensive dioceses. Bishops Eligius, Amandus, Lambert, and Hubert are closely connected with the religious history of Belgium in the seventh and eighth centuries. The boundaries of the dioceses corresponded exactly with the limits of the old administrative circles of the Roman Empire, the provinces. In the eighth century, Belgium was divided into the dioceses of Noyon-Tournai, Térouanne (later Saint-Omer), Arras, Cambrai, Liège, and Utrecht. The dioceses of Utrecht and Liège were subject to the metropolitan church of Cologne, the others to the metropolitan church of Rheims.

These dioceses had been established without taking into account the racial differences existing between the inhabitants of the ecclesiastical territory. Including in the same diocese Gallo-Romans and Franks, the church, unconsciously of course, prepared the inhabitants of Belgium for the task of being intermediaries between the Latin and the Teutonic civilization. The seats of the bishoprics being mostly located in the Romance section of the country, the inhabitants of the Teutonic section were obliged to meet the Walloons: they had the same religious center. As a result of this action of the church, the national or racial differences were diminished and the linguistic frontier no more operated as a barrier in any real sense between the people it separated.

If the conversion to the Catholic faith was mainly the task of the missionaries, the introduction of civilization was mainly the task of the monasteries. Here the Benedictine monks played a very large part, both as civilizers and as colonizers. Their monasteries were, from the sixth century on, centers of economic and intellectual life. While some of their monks attacked the thick forests of Southern and Central Belgium with axes, others engaged in literary labors in the monasteries' libraries, transcribing the ancient Greek and Latin manuscripts, composing hymns and Lives of Saints, and opening schools for the education of the people. They planted in the very hearts of the people the roots of that strong religious spirit, which has steadily developed, and which has become one of the characteristics of the national spirit of Belgium.

Each monastery became a kind of model farm, where the population of the neighborhood could learn the best agricultural methods. In the monastery, too, they could find physicians who knew how to take care of the sick. The monastery, being protected by the respect that was inspired by the saint to whom it was dedicated, was also a place of safety in time of danger. Consequently, dwellings became more and more numerous around the monasteries, and villages developed under their influence and protection.

It is not, then, surprising that in the course of time tales and legends developed wherein the founders of those monasteries became the heroes of poetical and sometimes extraordinary adventures. In this manner did the people of mediaeval times express their gratitude for all they owed to those early pioneers of culture and civilization.

CHAPTER II

THE PERIOD OF FEUDALISM

Charles the Great died in 814. His son, Emperor Louis, was a weakling, and after his death the mighty empire of Charles was destroyed by internal troubles and civil war (840). Lotharius, the youngest son of Emperor Louis, endeavored to seize the empire for himself. To prevent this, both his brothers, Louis and Charles, leagued themselves against him and defeated him in the terrible battle of Fontanet, which has been characterized by contemporaries as a "judgment of God." The peace that was later concluded between the three brothers led to the famous Treaty of Verdun (843), an event of the utmost importance in the history of Belgium.

The empire created by Charles the Great was divided into three parts: the central part, including the largest portion of Belgium, Holland, Italy, and the eastern part of France, was allotted to Lotharius, together with the title of Emperor; the western part of the empire, embracing the largest part of France, and Flanders to the west of the Scheldt, became the share of Charles; the eastern part, which included nearly the whole of Germany and certain parts of Austria-Hungary, was given to Louis. The Treaty of Verdun practically cut the territory of Belgium into two parts, separated by the Scheldt, and gave each of them to a different ruler. These two sections of Belgium remained separated during the Middle Ages, and were not reunited until six centuries later.

After the death of Emperor Lotharius (855) the northern part of his central territory, located between the North Sea and the Jura Mountains, was given to one of his sons, Lotharius II. That section which included the entire eastern part of Belgium to the Scheldt embraced peoples of very different race and origin: Frisians, Franks, Alamans, Walloons. As it was impossible to name the territory after its inhabitants—they were of too many different origins—it was named after its sovereign: *regnum Lotharii*, "Lotharingia," "the realm of Lotharius."

In 870 the Treaty of Meerssen, whereby Charles, King of France, and Louis, King of Germany, divided between them the realm of Lotharius II, ended the existence of that state. The second Treaty of Verdun in 879 finally settled the status of Lotharingia: the boundary between France and Germany was declared to be the river Scheldt, and the whole of Lotharingia was incorporated in Germany. Of course, all the parts of the former empire of Charles the Great were once again united by the Emperor Charles the Stout, but after all kinds of internal struggles, Lotharingia was again—and this time for many centuries—annexed to Germany in 925.

Belgium is thus divided into two tracts by the Scheldt: the western part, Flanders, belonging to France and politically influenced by that country; the eastern part, Lotharingia, which was a dependency of Germany. As in the establishment of the bishoprics, so here, no attention was paid to the racial differences of the inhabitants. Both Lotharingia and Flanders included peoples of different origin: Flanders had inhabitants of Teutonic origin in the north and inhabitants of Romance origin in the south; Lotharingia included Flemings in the east, the center, and the north, and Walloons in the south.

Thus, at the beginning of the feudal system, there existed no political and no linguistic unity in Belgium. Moreover, although Flanders formed a politically united body, Lotharingia was subdivided into several small principalities: the duchy of Brabant, including the actual provinces of Brabant and Antwerp, the county of Limburg, the county of Namur, the duchy of Luxemburg, the county of Hainaut, and two ecclesiastical principalities, Cambrai and Liège.

The absence of political unity was a consequence of the new political constitution of most of the countries of Western Europe in the tenth century—of feudalism, so called. In place of the former despotic and centralized power of the King there was now to be found the locally asserted rule of dukes, counts, viscounts, etc. These public officers who, in the ninth century, were still subordinate agents of the King, without any other power than that delegated to them by their master, had succeeded, partly through the weakness of the heirs of Charles the Great and partly on account of the invasions of the Normans in the ninth century and the incursion of the Hungarians in the tenth, in grasping more firmly their delegated powers and in making their military, political, and financial perquisites hereditary. Thanks to the custom whereby the King granted them a domain, called *beneficium*, as a reward for their services or to insure their loyalty, they had succeeded in getting a strong political foothold in their respective provinces, and had continuously developed their possessions and their influence. In the tenth century the dukes and counts, formerly officers of the King, had won for themselves an independent and hereditary position. The kingdom was now everywhere broken up into small principalities, practically autonomous, where the King no longer exercised his power and where the people were now dominated by local dynasties. The new political organization, called feudalism, existed, of course, in Belgium also, and contributed in a large measure to the complete absence of political and national unity throughout the country.

Each county, each duchy, became a world apart, had its own politics and made war on the neighboring principality, or aided it in case of attack from others. So Flanders enjoyed friendly relations with Cambrai and Hainaut; Hainaut was on good terms with Namur and Luxemburg. Sometimes they fought one another: Brabant and Limburg were enemies for a long time. Later they became united under the same princes. The same phenomenon existed in the Northern Netherlands: Holland was friendly toward Cleves, but fought against Gueldre on account of Utrecht, against Flanders on account of Zealand, against Utrecht on account of Friesland, etc.

For the most part, Flanders or the western part of Belgium was a vassal of the French King; Lotharingia or the eastern part of Belgium was a vassal of the German Empire. The dependency of Lotharingia, however, was less definite than was that of Flanders to France, for the numerous principalities into which the former was broken up introduced more autonomy for the local dynasties and rendered intervention on the part of the Emperor more difficult. Flanders, on the other hand, as a more homogeneous territory, was more closely united with its feudal lord.

The ultimate fate of Flanders and Lotharingia depended, however, on the degree of independence that their princes would be able to win. In accordance with the general politics of all vassals, the counts of Flanders and the dukes of Lotharingia dreamed of but one thing, namely, of escape from the domination of their feudal lord. The result was that, after some centuries, both parts of Belgium were brought more and more closely together, and from this resulted that much-needed political unity, the only hope of a real independent Belgium.

The political history of the country in feudal times (the tenth to the twelfth century) must now be examined.

Annexed to the German Empire, Lotharingia became from 925 a sort of German province, especially during the reign of Emperor Otto I (962), a man of powerful personality. Otto clearly realized that no layman at the head of Lotharingia would be loyal enough to submit entirely to his own politics and he therefore appealed to the devotion and faithfulness of the bishops. These were to be the agents of the German influence and domination. In 953 Otto appointed his own brother, Bruno, as Duke of Lotharingia and obtained for him at the same time the archbishopric of Cologne. Having thus acquired control of both the political and ecclesiastical power, Bruno became the intermediary by whom not only the duchy but also the Lotharingian church was to be more and more Germanized.

However, the domination of the imperial German church did not succeed in breaking entirely the resistance of the local Lotharingian princes. Those princes had no affection for the Emperor of Germany; they could not forget their old national dynasty, the Carolingians, who belonged to the country and were not foreigners, as were the German emperors. The people of Lotharingia supported those local dynasties which claimed descent from the old Carolingian national stock; the castles of the local counts of Hainaut, Louvain, and Limburg became centers of political influence, whose object was to check the domination of the feudal German lord. Since the tenth century the local houses of Hainaut and Louvain, of Namur and Luxemburg, had attempted to organize their political power. In the last quarter of the eleventh century, the Germanization of Lotharingia broke down as a result of the so-called "Struggle for the Investitures," whereby the power of the Emperor over the church in Germany was destroyed. The bishops of the Empire, having to choose between loyalty to their feudal lord and obedience to the pope, were no longer political servants of the Emperor. The downfall of the imperial church meant the end of its influence in Lotharingia. The local princes threw off the feudal yoke and practically divided the whole of Lotharingia among themselves. And thus was witnessed the end of that large imperial province that for so long had covered the western frontier of Germany between the Rhine and the Scheldt. We hear no more of Lotharingia: another name appears in Belgian history, namely, Brabant. It was the Duke of Brabant, of the local house of Louvain, who, from this time on, gradually extended his political influence over the former Lotharingia, in that part of Belgium lying east of the Scheldt.

The German Emperor was now no more the lord of the Lotharingian princes: he was henceforth regarded as an ally or as an enemy, according to the circumstances. The Lotharingian principalities no longer played a part in events occurring on the other side of the Rhine; they no longer sent soldiers to the feudal imperial army; they followed the emperors no more in their expeditions against Italy; and, in the Lotharingian literature, there is to be found hardly a suggestion of a recollection of the existence of the German Emperor.

From the middle of the twelfth century on, the national life of the eastern part of Belgium displayed more and more cohesion and individuality; little by little it broke down the geographical barrier of the Scheldt that the Treaty of Verdun had erected between Lotharingia and Flanders.

Meanwhile the western part of Belgium, the county of Flanders, had developed also in its own way. Assigned by the Treaty of Verdun to the kingdom of France, Flanders did not seek a separation from a country to which it was geographically attached and on whose territory were to be found the seats of its bishoprics and most of its monasteries. The political power of the house of Flanders dates from the time of Count Baldwin I, called Baldwin of the Iron Arm (879), an adventurous ruler, who violently took the daughter of the King of France, his lord, and made her his wife, notwithstanding the vehement protest of her royal father. That marriage brought to the count the rich possessions of his wife and furnished to his heirs an excellent pretext for meddling in the politics of France. The kings of France at the time of the first counts of Flanders were weaklings; moreover, the bishops of Noyon-Tournai, Arras, and Térouanne were not as loyal to their lord as those of Lotharingia were to the Emperor. The political conditions were thus quite different in Flanders, and at a time when the iron policy of Otto I and his heirs

subdued the Lotharingian princes, the counts of Flanders
succeeded in developing their independence and political
influence without much opposition. Baldwin II (910)
enlarged his domain by conquering the wealthy regions of
Walloon-Flanders[1] and Artois and formed an alliance with
England by marrying an Anglo-Saxon princess.   Count
Arnulf (918) took the title of marquess and tried—though
vainly—to overpower the Duke of Normandy, who
checked his advance in the south and with it the extension
of Flemish conquest beyond the river Canche.   Effect-
ively blocked in their efforts to extend their power in the
south, the Flemish counts next turned their attention to
the north and the east.   Successively the islands of Zeeland, the "Four Métiers," and the county of Alost were
subjugated, although already under the feudal authority
of the German Empire.   The result was that the Count of
Flanders became at once a vassal of the King of France
and of the German Emperor.

By the conquest of the county of Alost, Count Baldwin V was enabled to cross the Scheldt and to advance into
Lotharingian territory.   The marriage of his son with a
princess of Hainaut resulted in uniting both Flanders and
Hainaut under the same dynasty.   Here again the barrier
erected by the Treaty of Verdun was broken down, and for
the first time political ties were established on both sides
of the Scheldt, between the two parts of Belgium.

Coincident with the first signs of a tendency to union
between Eastern and Western Belgium, Flanders began to
come into closer contact with foreign countries and powers.
As the son of Baldwin V had married the daughter of

---

[1] By Walloon-Flanders is to be understood the southern part of the
county, including the cities of Lille, Douai, and Béthune.

William the Conqueror, Duke of Normandy, many Flemish troops took part in the conquest of England by the Normans (1066), and these remained in the British Isles for purposes of colonization.   Diplomatic and commercial relations between Flanders and England were the happy result.   Under Count Robert (1070), Flanders came into contact with Denmark and with the court of Rome; a pilgrimage to Jerusalem undertaken by Robert brought him into touch with the Emperor of Constantinople, and the Count of Flanders happened to be the first prince of Europe to consider a crusade against the Turks.

In the twelfth century, however, the political expansion of Flanders came to a standstill.   To the weaklings of the former period in France there had now succeeded kings of stronger character, whose policy led them to subdue their restless vassals and to centralize their own power.   They sought, therefore, to check the expansion of Flanders and to dominate the powerful county, attaching it more closely to the French domain.   The road to the south was thus no longer open for eventual conquest; the road to the east also was barred by the Lotharingian princes.   The influence of the German Empire had practically disappeared in Lotharingia.   Brabant and Hainaut now became the centers of a strong political life.   It is a curious phenomenon of history that, when Flanders was threatened by the growing strength of France, Lotharingia became practically independent of the influence of the German Empire.

There was, therefore, as has been seen, no political unity in Belgium during the feudal period: east and west each developed in its own way and political conditions in each section were very strongly influenced by their powerful neighbors. There did exist, however, a common tendency toward autonomy and freedom, Flanders trying to escape from the influence of France and, to some extent, that of England;[1] Lotharingia struggling against the hegemony of Germany. That tendency, it must be admitted, is not a purely characteristic Belgian movement. At this period the feudalists were everywhere to be found fighting against the supremacy of the King and trying to win complete political independence for themselves.

The one essentially Belgian factor in the diverging existence of the east and the west, and which exerted a strong influence in favor of unification, was the common social, economic, and religious life.

A study of religious conditions in Belgium during the tenth and eleventh centuries reveals, even more clearly than a study of political events, the part played by both Germany and France in imposing their respective practices, and the ability of Belgium to incorporate and to modify the best elements of Teutonic and Latin civilization.

After the Norman invasions of the ninth century, which left Belgium covered with ruins and with many churches and monasteries burned, or abandoned by their terrified occupants, the ecclesiastical discipline suffered severely. The old prescriptions of the Benedictine rule were no longer observed and most of the monasteries became dependents of powerful laymen.

In the tenth century a revival of the discipline followed, thanks to the efforts of St. Gerard of Brogne, founder of

---

[1] During the reign of Count Robert (1093), William the Conqueror, then King of England, adopted a hostile attitude toward Flanders. As a result Robert gave his daughter in marriage to the King of Denmark and, in agreement with him, planned an invasion of England. The hostile attitude of the English kings of the Norman dynasty turned the counts of Flanders to seek again the protection of France.

the little monastery of Brogne, near Namur (923). Gerard excited so much enthusiasm by the sanctity of his life and the rigor of his discipline that princes and bishops united in asking him to restore the practice of ascetic life both in Lotharingia and in Flanders. The number of the monasteries to the north of the linguistic barrier, especially in Flanders, soon increased, whereas before they were mainly to be found in Southern Belgium. Belgium became a country of monasteries in the eleventh century, and ever since that time the people have shown that deep religious spirit that is one of the distinctive traits of the national character. The monks exerted a very strong influence on the minds of the rough feudalists, who thought mainly of war and robbery: one of the most powerful dukes of Lotharingia, Godefrid the Bearded, desired to be buried in the dress of a monk. The robber-knights, pursuing an enemy or a convoy of merchants, thought only of plunder; once in sight of the walls of a monastery, however, they would cease their pursuit and turn back. Carrying through the country the relics of their saints, the monks would often succeed in stopping private wars and murder. An example of the religious spirit is the great "procession" of Tournai, that attracted every year thousands of pilgrims and visitors, Flemish and Walloon together, and that acted as a unifying factor for both races of Belgium.

The Reform of Cluny found the French and German influence in serious conflict. The reform in question, by which it was hoped to reintroduce a very severe discipline in the monastic world, originated in Lorraine (1004) and soon spread through the northern countries, especially in Flanders and Lotharingia. The monks of Cluny resolutely resented any interference of the temporal power in religious affairs. As a result they found themselves practically opposed to the system of the imperial and feudal church of Germany, dominated by the Emperor. The destruction of that system thus meant indirectly the destruction of German influence in Lotharingia. When the Struggle for the Investitures broke out, the Lotharingian bishops hesitated at first, but after a while nearly all of them took sides with the papal cause against the Emperor. Both in matters of politics and religion Lotharingia tended more and more to break away from Germany.

Hitherto only one monastic order had influenced religious life in Belgium, namely, the Benedictines. In the twelfth century other orders were born—the Cistercians and the Norbertins or Premontrés. The Cistercians, founded by St. Bernard in France, played the part, mainly, of clearers of wild land and of colonizers; they introduced new economic and agricultural methods and exerted a deep influence in economic life. The Premontrés were canons, rather than monks, who passed their time in study and in administering the parishes. But they, too, did much for the colonization of the country, and they transformed into fruit-bearing land the barren soil of the Antwerp Campine.

The number of parishes increased in the course of the tenth and eleventh centuries. New chapels were founded in cases where the nearest parish church was too far removed, or where a number of people sufficient for the formation of a new parish were to be found dwelling close together. Sometimes the establishment of a new parish was ordered at the instance of a wealthy landlord, and a

THE CATHEDRAL OF TOURNAI

chapel constructed on the domain of his manor, in order to gratify his desire for better opportunities for attending church. Each chapel was ordinarily granted the right to have its own parish priest, to whom was granted permission to baptize infants and bury the dead in the parish cemetery.

As for the economic organization, in ante-feudal times there existed an important difference between the country south and that lying north of a line drawn through Boulogne, Saint-Omer, Douai, Mons, and Maestricht. North of this line we find the system of isolated farms; south of the line the system of villages. But during the tenth century the landlords extended their possessions in farm lands as well as in the villages, and the same economic organization, directed by the same principles, prevailed throughout the country. Each domain was divided into two parts: a central part, including the manor of the landlord and that portion of the land exploited by himself by means of unfree "serfs" or agricultural laborers; and another part, surrounding the central domain, divided into small lots, given to free farmers.

The domain of the ecclesiastical landlords, bishops or abbots, was exceedingly well administered and the conditions of life of the people depending upon these landlords were very favorable; the ecclesiastical "serfs" frequently asserted that they preferred their servitude to freedom, as less burdensome than freedom itself. The ecclesiastical "serfs" were grouped in families, *familiae*, within whose limits justice was administered by the mayor of the community in the name of the abbot.

The lay landlords, on the other hand, were bad administrators. Dealing only with politics and war, they ignored agricultural problems; they did not come into contact with their laborers, and they left with their officers, *ministeriales*, the care of ruling and judging their servants. They preferred attendance at "tournaments," which might be regarded as a sort of military training and as a means of learning the profession of bearer of arms. They undertook long and distant journeys in order to fight the knights of Vermandois, Champagne, and Picardy in France. And as a result both Walloons and Flemings came in contact with their French brethren in arms.

The upper landlords, the dukes and counts, gave much attention, however, to the colonization and the economic improvement of the country. Northern and Western Flanders and Northern Brabant were covered with sandy soil and marshes, and thick woods were to be found in some parts as late as the end of the eleventh century. In the early part of that century, the counts of Flanders began to engage the unemployed for agricultural purposes. They turned the unproductive parts of the country into fertile meadows, suitable for pasturing cattle. Canals and dykes were constructed in order to increase the productivity of the soil. In the course of the twelfth century a sturdy populace of land laborers was attracted into Germany by the landlords of the countries of Bremen, Holstein, Thuringia, and Silesia. It was the Flemings and the people of Brabant who colonized the right bank of the river Elbe and who turned the marshes of Eastern Germany into fertile soil. Many villages still remind us today of those Flemings, and are still known as *Flämingdörfer*.

On the Flemish seacoast the people were engaged in raising cattle, especially sheep and cows; another large element was employed in herring and cod fishing in the North Sea. These people were mostly of Frisian or Saxon origin; they were not descendants of the Franks. They spoke another language; they had other customs and laws; they were socially free men. When the French influence increased in Flanders, they alone retained their Germanic characteristics, and it was among them, in the fourteenth century, that were found the fiercest opponents of France.

As affecting the artistic life of Belgium in the tenth and eleventh centuries, we find the same influences at work which have been mentioned as operative in political and religious spheres. The Romance and Germanic ideas were absorbed, mixed, and transformed by the Belgian artists of that time.

Lotharingia, the eastern part of Belgium, possessed, of course, no cathedrals comparable with those of Worms, Speyer, and Mainz. However, the literary movement developed by the Lotharingian bishops was accompanied by an artistic revival. As most of the Lotharingian bishops were of German descent, the direction of the work was intrusted to German architects. The oldest examples of romantic architecture in the regions of the Meuse reveal German influence. Not only the architects, but also the sculptors, the painters, etc., were Germans, though sometimes recourse was had to Italian artists, who came over the Alps to seek their fortunes. The frescoes on the walls of St. James's Church at Liège are the work of a painter called Giovanni.

The Lotharingian artists soon began to imitate the German methods and to use material native to the country. Supplies for walls and columns were no longer brought from Germany, but from the valley of the Meuse. Until the twelfth century, German traditions, however, prevailed in architecture, and at no time prior to the beginning of that period can there be said to have been any Lotharingian style.

If the valley of the Meuse was the artistic center of Eastern Belgium, in the western part of the country—in Flanders—it was the city of Tournai which dominated artistic development. The cathedral of Tournai, the only large Romance basilica of Belgium, rivals the cathedrals of the Rhine in majesty and harmony of form. The plan reveals the work of an architect influenced by the German school. But in the architectural details are to be found motifs inspired by the large French cathedrals of Normandy. The double German and French influence resulted in the founding of a local school of architecture at Tournai, which exhibited great activity throughout Flanders. Tournai, the religious capital of Flanders, became also the artistic capital. The stone of Tournai was famous. Thanks to the Scheldt, material was easily transported, and in the locality where it was used it was, of course, architects of Tournai who drew the plans of the buildings. There existed also at Tournai a local school of sculptors, whose members were very active and who may be regarded as true artists.

There remains only the literary life in both parts of Belgium during the feudal period to be considered.

Dating from the ninth century, there were many to be found among the ecclesiastics and the upper classes who spoke both languages, Romance and Teutonic, equally well. In the monasteries Flemish and Walloon monks lived together, and in the Abbey of St. Amand, in Southern

Belgium, there has been found, written by the same hand, the oldest poem of French literature, the *Cantilène de Ste. Eulalie,* and also one of the oldest products of Teutonic literature, the *Ludwigslied.* The bishops and abbots knew both languages; the abbots of Lobbes, a Walloon monastery in the tenth century, spoke both Flemish and French.   In the diocese of Térouanne (later Saint-Omer) the bishops were obliged to know "barbarian," i.e., the Teutonic language.   During the eleventh century, many preachers were able to address the people of the Walloon and Flemish sections, and abbots who knew both languages were preferred.   The lay princes were obliged at least to understand Walloon and Flemish, for Flanders, Brabant, and Limburg included people of both races. When the army of the crusaders started for the Holy Land, the Lotharingian prince Godfrid of Bouillon was appointed as their leader, because, according to the chronicle of Otto von Freising, "brought up on the frontier of the Romance and the Teutonic people, he knew both languages equally well."   During the twelfth century, the knowledge of French was regarded as a necessary element of perfect culture.   On the common people, however, French civilization had no influence at all; they knew and spoke only Flemish.

The French influence was especially strong from a linguistic point of view; the German influence was overwhelming in the literary domain, especially in Lotharingia.   The bishops were, generally speaking, the sole possessors of literary and scientific culture, and in Lotharingia most of them were strongly Germanized.   The center of literary life in Lotharingia was the school of Liège, founded by the Saxon bishop Everachar.   It became a center of study, where not only Germans, but also French, English, and Slav students were to be found. The curriculum of the school, known as the school of St. Lambert, included grammar, rhetoric, poetry, music, mathematics, and theology. This institution was the means by which many new ideas were circulated through France and Germany, as its teachers were in close touch with all the scientific tendencies of the time. In Western and Southern Belgium we find the influence of the school of Cambrai as paramount. Although a Romance region, Cambrai belonged to the German Empire, and was therefore a center of German influence. The dominating *genre* in literature is history, and that is an especially Belgian *genre;* history has always been much cultivated in Belgium. The historical work of a monk, Sigebert of Gembloux, is recognized as the center of that activity.

The Struggle for the Investitures, which destroyed the power and the influence of the German imperial and feudal church from a political and religious point of view, destroyed also its influence in literary life. The schools of Liège were abandoned and, from the first quarter of the twelfth century on, students turned their eyes toward Paris.

In Flanders, literary influence, as was the case with artistic movements, was French rather than German. Tournai, the artistic capital, was also the intellectual center, and Tournai was a Romance bishopric. The school of St. Mary had only French teachers and contributed in spreading a knowledge of the French language among the Flemish clergy. Essentially theological and dialectical, however, the teaching of St. Mary was less important than the teaching of St. Lambert of Liège.

Thus, during the tenth and eleventh centuries, the civilization of Belgium was influenced by the culture of its powerful neighbors. Nevertheless, the elements of German and French civilization were not simply absorbed; they were transformed, adapted, and nationalized, and became a real part of the life of the nation.

CHAPTER III

THE RISE AND INFLUENCE OF THE COMMUNES

A new epoch opens with the twelfth century in the history of Belgium. The era is frequently called the "Time of the Communes," because the internal political life of the country, from then on, was dominated by the development of the free cities (communes) and of their municipal institutions. And it has been said that "in the part played by the cities since the twelfth century lies the best of the history of the Netherlands."

Until the rise of the communes, only two classes of people, the noblemen and the priests, were given any recognition. There remained, of course, the peasant farmers, but they had no political or social power. After the twelfth century, a new class sprang into existence— the burgesses (*bourgeois, burgers*), the citizens of the free cities—and the rise of that class exerted a tremendous influence on the political and social development of the nation. To the tyranny of feudalism it opposed the spirit of personal and collective freedom, and the social construction of the nation was materially influenced by the introduction of the new elements it represented.

The origin and development of the communes was mainly due to economic conditions: the Belgian cities of the Middle Ages were the daughters of trade and industry.

Beginning with the eleventh century many signs indicated a complete revival of trade, which had been

36

THE BELFRY OF GHENT
On the right the Town Hall

nearly annihilated by the internecine struggles and the invasion of the Normans during the ninth century. At the end of the tenth century Flanders was already in touch with the Arab merchants trading in the Baltic; coins of the counts of Flanders are to be found in Denmark, Prussia, and Russia. The merchants of that time were traveling merchants, going from one town to another, and never remaining permanently in any one spot. All along the rivers wharves were established for discharging goods and wares, as well as winter quarters for the traders for the period during which the rivers were frozen. These were to be found at Valenciennes, Cambrai, Ghent on the Scheldt, Dinant, Huy, Liège, and Maestricht on the Meuse. Bruges became a central meeting-place for Flemish, Walloon, German, Frisian, and Anglo-Saxon merchants, and between the Scheldt and the Thames commercial intercourse was frequent. Little by little there grew up a special class who depended for a living on sale and purchase. A man became a merchant just as another became a knight, a priest, or a farmer. All those without land, the discontented "serfs" who succeeded in escaping from the domain to which they were attached, steadily augmented this early nucleus of the merchant class.

The invasion of England by William the Conqueror (1066) and the large numbers of the Flemings who participated in it strengthened the economic ties between that country and Flanders, between London and Bruges. In Bruges[1] vessels from all parts of Europe were loaded with cargoes for London: wine from France and Germany,

---

[1] The outlet to the sea for the city of Bruges was by means of the river Zwyn.

stone from Tournai, cloth of gold and groceries sent by the merchants of Lombardy, wool and linen cloths manufactured in Flanders. The prosperity of the Flemish trade attracted the representatives of European commerce; fairs and yearly markets were established at Thourout, Messines, Lille, Ypres, and Douai.

Along with trade came the development of industry. On the Belgian coast the sheep-raising industry goes back as far as the early days of Roman occupation; woolen cloths were a special manufacture of the region. The more extensive the "polders"—the meadows wrested from the sea—became, the more the number of sheep raised on them increased, and consequently also the number of people connected with the wool industry. As trade developed the conditions of that industry, more and more people found occupation in the manufacture of woolen cloths. A special class of craftsmen was born. They deserted the countryside and settled down in the neighborhood of the merchants; trade and industry attracted each other. Flanders then became the seat of the cloth industry.

Another kind of industry was in process of development in Eastern Belgium, in the valley of the Upper Meuse. This was a mountainous region, filled with copper and tin mines along the banks of the river between Huy and Dinant. Here was developed a metal industry, whose products were shipped out on the river Meuse. After the tenth century the native mines were no longer sufficient for the needs of the country; the population of Huy and Dinant supplied its needs from the mines of Goslar in Germany. The products of the copper and tin industry were exported to France and England.

Brabant, the central part of Belgium, remained for a long time purely agricultural. In the middle of the twelfth century, however, a highroad was constructed between Cologne and Bruges, passing through Maestricht, Saint-Trond, Léau, Louvain, Brussels, Alost, and Ghent. Trade now flowed, not only from south to north by the Scheldt and the Meuse, but also from east to west along the new commercial road.

This remarkable development of trade and industry was mainly responsible for the origin and growth of the communes. Of course, for many centuries episcopal residences (*civitates*), castles and manors (*castra*), churches and monasteries had been centers of civilization and an attraction for the population of the neighborhood. And under the protection of their walls were grouped many wealthy villages. The latter, however, would probably never have developed into cities except for the presence of a colony of merchants and craftsmen. These colonies established themselves in neighborhoods where they could find favorable conditions for trading as well as protection for their commerce. Naturally, therefore, they settled in the vicinity of castles and convents (the castles affording military and the convents moral protection), at the confluence of two or more rivers, along a commercial highroad, in the curve of a gulf, or at the mouth of a stream. In this manner the cities of Bruges, Ghent, Brussels, Louvain, Liège, Malines, etc., were born, for it is an interesting point of Belgian history that nearly all the cities originated during the Middle Ages, very few of them dating back to the Roman times. Those colonies of merchants and craftsmen grouped together in professional and religious associations were called "guilds," and introduced an entirely new spirit among the people of the growing town. The unfree population dependent upon the convent, the church, or the castle had no means of changing its conditions of life, bound as it was by the numerous ties of feudal and other obligations. But the traders had to secure for themselves a certain degree of liberty, safety, and autonomy. The feudal régime or the rules of the manor were intolerable to them. The operation of the system was too tyrannous; it acted too much as a restraint on private liberty and would have rendered the free development of commercial and industrial enterprises impossible.

The guilds, therefore, formerly purely professional associations, soon began to meddle in politics and to become political organizations as well. Their members discussed in their guild-halls, built for their business meetings, the changes desired in the existing social, economic, and political conditions of the community, and carried on propaganda in support of their demands.

At the same time the members of the guilds began to build walls around the settlement, in order to protect the new city against attack from the outside. Such a fortified town was called *burgus, bourg,* "borough," and the inhabitants were called *burgenses, bourgeois,* "burgesses."

When the burgesses began to work for changes in the existing régime of the territory in which the town had developed, the princes and landlords to which that territory belonged naturally showed opposition. In some cases they resisted the demands of the guild, but the people were frequently induced to rebel and, by a revolutionary method, to wrest from their overlords the rights they demanded. In most cases the princes recognized the justice of the claims and granted the burgesses a new law, better suited to the needs of commerce and industry. This new law, the city law, different from the feudal law and the law of the manor, was called *Keure* in Flemish, *charte de commune* in French. It contained the political, social, and financial privileges granted by the landlord and the prince to the burgesses. When the city law was granted, the commune came into existence. One of the most important privileges of the commune was a special tribunal, called *échevinage, schepenbank*, composed of citizens and presided over by an officer appointed by the lord.

The commune possessed political and judicial autonomy and its inhabitants were personally free. A man from a neighboring country or a foreigner who had dwelt in the city for one year and one day became a burgess and enjoyed all the privileges of citizenship. Although politically autonomous, the commune still owed certain obligations to its lord. These were mainly an oath of allegiance and the duty of assisting the lord with its army of citizens. This latter duty sometimes created curious situations. At the battle of the Golden Spurs in 1302, when King Philip IV of France was defeated by the Flemish communists, the inhabitants of Louvain fought on the side of the French King against their Flemish brethren, because their lord, the Duke of Brabant, was a partisan of Philip.

Although the commune owed certain duties to the lord, it had also, as a politically autonomous body, some important rights: the right to have a special seal to be appended to the official documents issued by the commune; the right to build a city hall and a belfry, the belfry being a tower, usually erected in the market-place, where the bell that called the burgesses to arms was hung, and where the archives of the city were care-fully kept in iron safes. As the commune exercised the right of life and death over its members, it erected as symbols of that right the pillory and the gallows, generally at the gate or outside the city wall.

The development of the communes was not quite the same in the various sections of Belgium. In the princi-pality of Liège, the cities of Dinant, Huy, and Saint-Trond obtained their privileges sooner than Liège itself. The charter of freedom for Huy dates from 1066. In the ecclesiastical principality of Cambrai the commune was established by violently revolutionary means in 1077. The merchants of Cambrai suffered from the tyranny of the officers appointed by the bishops, and a conspiracy was organized. On a certain day when Bishop Gerard left the town, the citizens ran to arms, under the leadership of the prominent merchants, and proclaimed the com-mune. But the bishop returned unexpectedly and his knights killed many of the people and pillaged the houses of the leaders. The supremacy of the bishop was restored for a long period.

In Flanders, the counts were sincere protectors of the communes; they regarded them as a mighty resource of their treasury and early recognized the claims of the *mercatores*. From the end of the eleventh century the main demands contained in the propaganda of the guilds were accepted and special privileges were granted to the cities. From the time of Count Charles the Good (1119-27), each city had its own *échevins* (sheriffs), chosen from among the burgesses; the president alone, the *bailli*, was

an officer of the lord, and responsible only to him.   The
house of the counts of Alsace (1128) owed its accession
to the communes and therefore protected the cities in a
special manner.   They gave to all of them the same
municipal charter, a copy of the charter of Arras, and
both the Flemish and the Walloon communes of Flanders
enjoyed identically the same privileges.

In the duchy of Brabant, the communes developed
more slowly, owing to the fact that conditions for the
development of trade and industry were not so much
advanced here.   From the time when the commercial
highroad between Cologne and Bruges was constructed
the municipal movement was participated in more
actively by the princes.   Here, also, the princes came
to assume the same sympathetic attitude as in Flanders,
but there was no general organization granting the same
type of constitution for all the cities.   The privileges
of each city were recognized and granted separately.

The existence of the communes exerted a powerful
influence on the internal politics of the feudal lords of
Belgium.   The latter were forced to take the communes
more and more into account and to change their political
attitude in accordance with the wishes of the burgesses.
The knights, almost ruined by the decline of the value of
the land, rendered military service only when paid for it.
The feudal troops were no longer sufficient in numbers.
The princes were obliged to seek the aid of the cities, to
beg for taxes in order to pay the loans they were now
obliged to contract for the allowances of the mercenary
troops which they were compelled to hire.   The princes
no longer governed alone; they had to respect and
cultivate the friendship of the cities.   Their subjects

began to take part in the political combinations of the feudalists. As a matter of fact, war was no longer possible without the consent of the communes, and it resulted, therefore, that the burgesses, if in disagreement with their lord, instead of assisting him, appealed to foreign rulers and fought against their own prince. It may be said that, owing to these changes in political life, the communes had succeeded in breaking the régime of feudalism. This may be cited as a supreme instance of their importance in Belgian history.

No less important was the influence they exerted—mainly during the thirteenth century—in the development of the economic, industrial, social, intellectual, and artistic life of the country. During that period trade and industry were essentially prominent in the life of the people. On account of their excellent location, the Belgian seaports became the meeting-places of vessels from the North Sea, the Baltic, the Mediterranean, the Orient. Ever since the existence of the commercial highroad between Cologne and Bruges the trade of the former had declined more and more. Given a shorter route by land, it is, generally speaking, that which is selected by merchants by which to forward their goods. Ghent became the center of commercial relations between Flanders and Germany, and many privileges were granted to Ghent tradesmen. Antwerp also grew little by little into an important commercial center, being connected with the Cologne-Bruges road by means of the Scheldt, that joins that road at Ghent.

Bruges, however, remained the commercial metropolis. It was in direct contact with the sea. Located midway between the Sunt and the straits of Gibraltar, it stored

goods arriving from the north and from the south. A
new harbor was constructed at Damme and connected
with Bruges by a canal, whose powerful moles have been
immortalized by Dante in his *Divina Comedia*.[1] The
market-place at Bruges was crowded as much as was
the Piazza San Marco in Venice. Toward the middle of the
thirteenth century Bruges was enjoying trade relations
with England, Normandy, Gascony, Spain, Provence,
and the Hanseatic cities. In the fourteenth century
the development of the harbor reached its climax by the
organization of a regular transport service between the
Flemish port and Genoa and Venice.

The growth of Flemish commerce was increased by
the liberal free exchange policy of the counts of Flanders,
especially since the time of Baldwin IX (1202). There
was no taking advantage of foreign trade, no heavy taxes,
no stringent customs. Many privileges were granted
to the "Osterlings," the merchants from Germany. If a
war broke out between Flanders and a Hanseatic city, the
Osterlings were allowed a period of three months in which
to leave the country and to put their belongings in safety.
The same privileges were granted to merchants from
Poitou, Gascony, and Spain.

Necessarily, also, Bruges became a center of financial
operations: pawnbrokers from Cahors, Lombardy, Florence, and Sienna flocked to the city in large numbers and
soon monopolized all credit operations. The Lombardic
pawnbrokers, especially, invaded the whole country
between the Meuse and the sea, and it is an astonishing
fact that in small cities like Léau (in the neighborhood of
Louvain) branch offices of the mighty banking houses

---

[1] *Inferno*, XV, 4–6.

of Paris were to be found. The important part played by the circulation of money is also proved by the many coin reforms of that time. The Belgian coins, owing to their excellence and high standard, were imitated in Germany by the Hanseatic cities.

At the time of the communes manufacture was even more important than trade. The Belgian provinces became essentially an industrial country: from Douai to Saint-Trond there is not a city which was not connected with the cloth industry. Belgian textures became unequaled in suppleness, delicacy, and beauty of color; they were to be found everywhere throughout Europe, and were exported even to the bazaars of the Orient by vessels from Venice, Marseilles, and Barcelona. It is in the south of Flanders that the art of dyeing seems to have reached the highest perfection. Ypres, Douai, with its famous *écarlate*, and Arras are especially entitled to mention in this particular. The cloth industry was soon introduced farther north, in Ghent and Bruges, and also in Brabant. Brussels, Malines, and Louvain early rivaled the Flemish cities.

The annexation of Walloon Flanders by France deprived the Flemish cloth industry of one of its sources of raw material, and it became necessary to obtain it from England. Since that time Flanders and England have been naturally dependent on each other and in this fact is to be found the reason for the close alliance between these countries, from a political point of view, especially in the fourteenth century. The commercial relations between Flanders and England were monopolized by a powerful association of wool importers, the Hansa of London, composed of Flemish tradesmen. After a

THE COLLEGIATE CHURCH OF SAINT GUDULA, BRUSSELS

while the cloth industry developed to such an extent that the supply of English wool was no longer sufficient: wool from Spain and Navarre was also employed.

Aside from the territory in which the cloth industry flourished, Belgium possessed also an agricultural region, far less developed, of which Hainaut was the center. Here the cities were merely large villages: Mons, Binche, and Ath cannot be compared with the cities of Flanders and Brabant. Namur and Luxemburg also were merely agricultural regions with no more than 8,000 and 5,000 population, respectively; whereas Ghent and Bruges had a populace of no less than 80,000, at least at the climax of their development.

In the valley of the Meuse, cities like Saint-Trond and Huy, where the cloth industry flourished in smaller degree, were unable to rival those of Flanders. The city of Dinant, on the Meuse, which, as stated before, was, from the end of the tenth century, engaged in the copper industry, may be singled out. The products of Dinant, called *dinanderie*, were exported throughout Europe. The merchants of Dinant had a storehouse in London and were members of the Hanseatic Association.

Finally, there remains the city of Liège in Eastern Belgium. This was a city of priests, the residence of the bishop-prince. It was filled with churches, convents, and chapels. The land was owned largely by religious communities. But the priests were more numerous than the burgesses.[1] There was no thought here of industry until the end of the Middle Ages, when this part of the country became the seat of collieries and ironworks.

---

[1] The priests and monks, as subject to the canon or ecclesiastical law, were not citizens. They were judged by their special tribunals, not by the *échevinage*.

Under the influence of such commercial and industrial conditions as we have recited, the life of the country people and the control of the soil were entirely transformed. After the twelfth century the old agricultural régime broke down and servitude became an exception; generally speaking, the peasant was thenceforward a free man, like the burgess. This important change came in connection with the crisis introduced by the new economic conditions of the twelfth century. At this time the value of money decreased rapidly and both the ecclesiastical and lay landlords found themselves threatened with bankruptcy. The methods of the old economic organization had to be changed if ruin was to be averted. New methods, therefore, were introduced by the Cistercian monks. The houses of this monastic order were very numerous at the beginning of the twelfth century; they constituted a class of an entirely new type. Most of their establishments were located among the marshes and heaths, which they were obliged to convert into fertile soil. For that work the monks alone were insufficient; they needed the help of so-called lay-brethren, who cultivated and fertilized the land. Round the monasteries themselves they established large farms, which became centers of new agricultural methods. The raising of cattle and the culture of corn were now their main business, and the crops were not merely intended for the consumption of the convent but a large part was sent to market to be sold. The peasants employed for this work were no longer "serfs," but free workers coming from outside. Servitude did not exist on the territory owned by the Cistercians. The monks soon became wealthy capitalists, but they utilized their means in clearing the heaths of the Campine, the forests of Hainaut, and in creating the "polders" of the Flemish coast. At the end of the thirteenth century the clearing of the land was finished and the farms and "polders" were rented out to free farmers. That system was likewise followed by the other monastic orders, and the class of free farmers soon grew more and more numerous. The example given by the Cistercians was followed by laymen. A large part of Brabant, Hainaut, Flanders, and Namur was covered with heaths, woods, and marshes. The dukes and counts, seeing what had been accomplished, began to order this wild land to be cleared. Along with the clearing of the soil came the foundation of new cities. The Belgian cities whose names contain the suffix -*sart*, -*rode*, or -*kerke*[1] date from this time. In order to get workers enough for clearing the land, the princes sought to attract them by granting special privileges, such as complete personal freedom and cession of land subject to a very small payment. A new type of peasant was born in Flanders—the peasant who was a freeman and who owned his own land. The peasants of Hainaut, Namur, and Ardennes were, of course, less in touch with the modern spirit; the different commercial and industrial conditions operated to keep them longer in servitude. Since the thirteenth century most of the Belgian peasants have been free, whereas in Germany servitude appeared even at the end of the Middle Ages.

As to the literary life and the respective positions of the French and Flemish languages at this time, the next chapter, which deals with the political conditions of Belgium in the period of the communes, will show the

[1] E.g., Rixensart, Baesrode, Middelkerke.

increasing influence of France, both in Flanders and in Brabant. It will not be surprising, therefore, to find that France exercised an influence upon Belgium from a literary and artistic point of view also. Flanders, a fief of France, was the first to feel that influence, and to feel it in a greater degree than any other Belgian principality. As a spoken language, French made a strong advance in the thirteenth century, albeit the conquest was a peaceful one. The wealthy communes of French or Walloon Flanders, like Arras, became real centers of French literature and culture. The Cistercians spread the knowledge of French in the monasteries, their order being originally French. The aristocracy also took part in the movement, following the example of the princes. The counts were all of Romance descent. The house of Alsace came from France; Baldwin VIII and Baldwin IX were Walloons; the countesses Jeanne and Marguerite were educated in Paris; the counts of the house of Dampierre came originally from Champagne. The language of the court as well as the language officially used was French. The wealthy burgesses sought to imitate the noblemen, and it was necessary for the merchants to know French to enable them to visit the fairs of Champagne.

However, we know that some of the commercial acts were written in Flemish. Flemish was overwhelmingly the popular tongue in Ghent and Bruges, and public officers were obliged to know and speak it, as well as French and Latin. As before, the common people remained faithful to the Flemish language; it was the only one they spoke. Flemish was also the principal language spoken in Brabant. Here the dukes strongly resisted French political hegemony, and Brabant remained the most independent Belgian province. French was, of course, made use of by the dukes in their private and domestic affairs, but Flemish prevailed in all their relations with their subjects; it was the language used by public officers. If the aristocracy was Gallicized, it was merely a matter of custom and *bon ton*.

As to the Romance literary movement, its productions were to be found in those regions where trade and industry tended to the increase of wealth. Luxemburg did not produce anything and Liège very little; in the latter city, moreover, the persons in the entourage of the bishop were largely German or Flemish. Romance literature flourished in Flanders, Brabant, and Hainaut; it was written in Picard, the original dialect that the writers themselves preferred, in opposition, so to speak, to French. The literature in question consisted partly of translations into the vernacular of Latin works written on science, partly of historical productions, and partly of poetry. The historical *genre* was much cultivated, but was more and more limited to castles and convents. Although the burgesses of the communes, eager to know as much as possible, found interest and pleasure in the historical writers (and it may be pointed out that the valuable chronicle of Philip Mousket was composed, about 1240, for the townspeople of Tournai), the citizens of the communes preferred the new *genre* introduced in literature, the *poésie bourgeoise*, wherein animals played a large part as personages; the *épopée* of *Rinehart the Fox* is particularly famous.

The rich development of Romance literature in Flanders and Hainaut prevented to some extent the early birth of an original and independent Flemish literature. Flemish literature had modest origins: it consisted at first merely of translations from the French, but it is highly interesting to note that it was through the intermediary of Flemish translations that French productions were introduced into Germany. The *Legend of Saint Servais* and the *Enéide*, composed by the Flemish knight, Hendrik Van Veldeke, following Latin sources, enjoyed an immense success and were promptly imitated in Germany. The French version of *Rinehart the Fox* was adapted in Flemish by a certain William, who surpassed his model, localized the story to the neighborhood of Ghent and the country of Waes, and gave to his work a real Flemish color.

The spirit of the Flemish burgesses, ordinarily inclined to be jeering and satirical, nevertheless inspired the greatest poet of thirteenth-century Flemish literature, Jacob Van Maerlandt, called "the father of all the Flemish poets." He founded in Flanders the didactical *genre*, adapted to the practical and sensible character of the nation. His object was to give to laymen access to the knowledge hitherto monopolized by the clergymen. His writings were in the field of natural history, politics and ethics, and sacred and profane history. He enjoyed great success and achieved the honor of seeing his works translated into French. Maerlandt, although he seemed to despise the French poets because he found their work too frivolous, was not a political writer. His greatness lay in the fact that he exercised a decisive influence on Flemish culture. He brought the Flemish language to the rank of a really literary language and developed it into an instrument capable of expressing the national genius. The soul of Flanders lives in Maerlandt's poems.

There yet remains to be considered the artistic development during the early period of the communes. French influence was prominent in the thirteenth century in the southern and western parts of the country. Tournai, of course, remained the artistic center of Flanders, and it was through Tournai that Gothic art was introduced into Belgium, just as Romantic art had earlier been introduced through Liège. The new choir of the cathedral of Tournai (*ca.* 1250) is remarkably French in its plan and methods of construction. But, on the whole, the school of Tournai does not merely copy the French style. It possesses its own originality; its type is full of charm and elegance. Its influence, thanks to the use so frequently made of the stone of Tournai, is overwhelming in Flanders, especially in Ghent and Bruges and in Hainaut.

Brabant, on the other hand, has a style of its own, owing to the fact that it uses its own local materials, found in its numerous quarries. There is a wide difference between the style of St. John's Church at Ghent and St. Gudula's Church at Brussels, although their choirs are nearly contemporaneous. In the course of the fifteenth century the school of Brabant became dominant.

In another region—that part of Flanders near the sea and known as "maritime Flanders"—stone from Tournai was not used because of the difficulty of access, and here there is also to be found an independence of style. There brick was made use of in place of stone, and, although the inspiration of the architecture came from Tournai, the style of that school underwent some change, owing to the difference in the materials employed. The houses of Bruges reveal the ornaments in brick peculiar to that style.

An entirely rich and original style, a sign of the power and the wealth of the communes, is to be found in the civic monuments, particularly the town halls. Everyone is familiar with the hall of Bruges and the magnificent hall of Ypres, a gem of beauty. With their wonderful belfries, their wide rooms, and the vast proportions of the edifices themselves, they symbolize in a wonderful manner the strength, the pride, and the glory of the Belgian cities in the Middle Ages.

THE SPLENDOR THAT WAS YPRES

Now destroyed by the German bombardments (Cloth Hall, Hôtel de Ville, and Cathedral)

CHAPTER IV

THE POLITICS AND STRUGGLES OF THE TIME
OF THE COMMUNES

A consideration of the politics of the Belgian dukes and counts during the course of the twelfth and the thirteenth centuries leads to a division of this epoch into two periods. During the twelfth century a policy of maintaining a balance between their mighty neighbors, France, England, and the Empire, was pursued. At the beginning of the thirteenth century France gained the hegemony in Europe, and the Belgian princes were forced to submit to the strong influence of that country.

In the first quarter of the twelfth century the Struggle for the Investitures had destroyed German influence in the eastern part of Belgium. The influence of the emperors was on the wane. One of the most loyal of the partisans of Emperor Frederick Barbarossa, the Count of Hainaut, succeeded in remaining neutral during the war between Germany and France. The Count declared that "he was not obliged to put his fortresses in the hands of the imperial troops and to grant them passage through his territory, as that would bring devastation to his country. His country being located between Germany and France, he ought to remain neutral during this war."

The unsympathetic attitude of the Lotharingian princes toward Germany, however, was not dictated by anything like national hostility or racial prejudice, for the Flemish principalities, with their inhabitants of Germanic descent, were as unfriendly as the Walloon principalities. It was

indifference, rather, for the Lotharingian princes had no
interests in common with the Empire. They went their
own way and had little regard for the Emperor. The
social and economic development of the country between
the Scheldt and the Meuse likewise prevented the people
of that region from sympathizing with Germany. The
culture of Germany, at this time a purely agricultural
country, was far behind the culture of the Belgian principalities. The Lotharingian princes turned their eyes
toward Flanders, with which they enjoyed important
commercial relations. On the other hand, the counts of
Flanders had sought, ever since the reign of Thierry of
Alsace (1168), to interfere with the countries across the
Scheldt and to meddle in the politics of Holland, Brabant,
Hainaut, Namur, Gueldre, and even Liège. Henceforth
the Belgian principalities, having common political and
economic interests, will be found to have an increasingly
common history. Thanks to its relations with Flanders,
Lotharingia now began to come into contact with France
and England.

Flanders, at this time, was very powerful. In 1163
Count Philip of Alsace had occupied, in the name of his
wife, the French counties of Vermandois, Amiénois, and
Valois, and had become the first vassal of the French
crown. But at that moment the throne of France was
occupied by a king of very strong personality, who himself directed the government of France and who had
decided to destroy the power of his restless vassals. That
king was Philip August. He directed his efforts especially against Flanders. He is quoted as having once
said: "France will absorb Flanders or will be destroyed
by it."

It was in vain that Count Philip of Alsace sought to win the support of the German Emperor. Having failed on this side, he turned to England for help against the threatening policy of his overlord. This was a highly important event (1187), for from that time on it became the constant policy of Flanders to keep England as an ally against France.

When Philip of Alsace died suddenly during the siege of Saint Jean d'Acre by the Crusaders, June 1, 1191, Philip August regarded this as a favorable opportunity to annex the county. He was prevented from doing so, however, by the action of the Count of Hainaut, Baldwin V, brother-in-law of the late Flemish count, who invaded Flanders and succeeded in bringing about the political union of the two counties. The county of Artois, however, refused to enter the union, and returned to Philip August. The latter hoped that, as Baldwin V (IX in Flanders) had only two daughters as his heirs, it would be easy to dispose of a strong political influence in the country after the death of Baldwin. Accordingly he brought about the marriage of Jeanne of Flanders, the eldest daughter of Baldwin,[1] to one of his creatures, Ferrand of Portugal. Henceforth he considered that Flanders would be in his hands. Subsequent events, however, were to prove his mistake.

When Count Ferrand arrived in Flanders he was met by the action of a strong feudal party, secretly supported by the subsidies of Philip August. He tried to escape the threatening French influence and, following the policy of his predecessors, appealed to England for help. Now

[1] Count Baldwin became Emperor of Constantinople and was killed by the Bulgarians after the battle of Adrianople (1205).

began a fierce struggle between French and English gold
for influence in the country. Moderately financed by
England, the partisans of the latter became stronger every
day. Finally Count Ferrand took a decided stand,
repudiated his allegiance to his overlord, and openly
accepted the English alliance. Just at this time a vast
coalition had been organized against the French king by
John I of England, Emperor Otto of Brunswick, and
Henry I, Duke of Brabant, with whom Ferrand of Flanders
joined. On July 27, 1214, the battle of Bouvines was
fought. The allies were defeated by Philip August;
Count Ferrand of Flanders fell into the hands of his feudal
lord, and was imprisoned at Paris.

The victory of Bouvines established the political
hegemony of France in Europe and the subjection of
Flanders. The former policy of balance was no longer
possible for the Belgian princes. In face of the overwhelming power of the French King, there remained
nothing but submission. From the date of the battle of
Bouvines to the beginning of the fourteenth century
Flanders was subject to the political and intellectual
domination of its strong neighbor.

The other Belgian principalities likewise shared the
ambition to win the friendship of the French King.
From now on the French monarchs found no occasion
for armed interference with the Belgian princes. Diplomacy met all needs, and agents from Paris, often shrewd
Italians, brought to the heads of the Belgian principalities the wishes—and orders—of their master.

Only one Belgian prince, the Duke of Brabant, resisted
the French influence. Since the former duchy of Lotharingia, at the beginning of the twelfth century, had been

broken up into many parts, Brabant became the leading power in the central part of Belgium. The house of the dukes of Brabant was indeed the only dynasty that could boast of its national origin; the other Belgian principalities all fell, during the thirteenth century, into the hands of new and foreign families. The dynasty of Brabant was thus exceedingly popular; it won the affection of the noblemen and of the communes, and the person of the duke was the object of real national affection. Moreover, the policy of the dukes was positive and practical, and, above all, paid due regard to the interests of their subjects. One of the main principles of this policy was the conquest of the commercial highroad between the Rhine and the sea, upon which the economic prosperity of Brabant depended.

As the principality of Liège and the county of Limburg blocked the road to the east, controlling all traffic between the Rhine and Bruges, after the reign of Henry I (1190) the dukes of Brabant turned their eyes in this direction. The war with Liège in Henry's time was not very successful. During the thirteenth century, therefore, the dukes sought to overpower Liège by a resort to diplomacy. As the bishop-prince of Liège was engaged in a continuous struggle against the communes, the dukes of Brabant sometimes supported the bishop against the burgesses, sometimes helped the latter against their lord, according to the needs of the moment.

Ever since 1283, when the Countess Ermengard of Limburg died without heirs, the dukes had cast covetous eyes on Limburg. Many pretenders, including several princes from the left bank of the Rhine, had sprung up. Duke John I of Brabant decided to strike the final blow against the coalition formed against him by the lords of Fauquemont, the Count of Luxemburg, Renaud of Gueldre, and the mighty Archbishop of Cologne. The coming battle would decide to whom should belong the supremacy between the Rhine and the Meuse. By skilful diplomacy, Duke John succeeded in preventing the Count of Flanders and the Bishop of Liège from allying themselves with his enemies. On June 5, 1288, the armies met at Worringen, on the Rhine. The battle lasted a whole day with terrific onslaughts. The army of Brabant, composed of the knights of the duchy, and the communal infantry from Louvain, Brussels, Antwerp, Tirlemont, Jodoigne, and Nivelles, although inferior in numbers to the foe, won a complete victory by the superiority of its tactics. It was a rout for Duke John's enemies. Twelve hundred of them fell on the battlefield, and both the Archbishop of Cologne and the Count of Gueldre were made prisoners, the Count of Luxemburg and his brothers being numbered among the slain. By sunset, the remainder of the enemy was in full flight and the trumpets of Brabant gaily proclaimed the victory.

The victory of Worringen had far-reaching consequences. It sealed the political decline of the archbishops of Cologne, who thenceforth interfered no more in Belgian affairs; Limburg was annexed by Brabant, and the latter extended its authority over the east of Lotharingia. The dukes now controlled the commercial road between Germany and the sea, and commanded the course of the Meuse, and since their sway encircled the principality of Liège, no further danger was to be feared in this quarter. The German Emperor made no protest against the annexation of Limburg, although it was actually territory of the

Empire. It was now perfectly clear that the influence of Germany in Eastern Belgium had come to an end.

This fact encouraged the kings of France to seek to occupy in Belgian affairs the place formerly occupied by Germany. But although the dukes of Brabant maintained peaceful relations with France, they had no wish to become simply the instruments of French politics. They resisted every attempt at domination. Henceforth Brabant, thanks to its spirit of independence, the strong and able diplomacy of its rulers, and the growing spirit of patriotism that characterized its people, became more and more the bulwark of Belgian liberty. It will be found hereafter as the very center of resistance to every attempt at foreign domination, and, in the sixteenth century, it was the States of Brabant which led the struggle against the tyranny of Spain.

At the time that the battle of Worringen strengthened the position of Brabant in Central and Eastern Belgium, a new king, Philip IV, called Philip the Fair, ascended the throne of France. His policy was to continue and complete the plans of Philip August, the strengthening of the central power at the expense of the grand vassals, and the subjection of Flanders to the crown.

The ruling count in Flanders at this time was Guy de Dampierre, whose family came originally from Champagne. Guy had become one of the most powerful princes of Belgium. Supported by the French King, he had successfully brought to an end a struggle with the hostile dynasty of the D'Avesnes in Hainaut, had annexed the county of Namur, and had won real influence in Liège, Luxemburg, and Gueldre. Philip the Fair soon began to fear the growing might of his vassal and decided to crush it.

The internal struggles in Flanders offered him an opportune pretext. In the beginning, it was only the wealthy, the merchants and owners of property, who exercised political power in the commune and who controlled the offices. Later on, the laboring classes, forming themselves into corporations, became powerful and claimed the right to control the administration of the communal finances and a share in the public offices. The wealthy—the patricians—resisted, endeavoring to maintain their preponderance. The result was a violent civil war between patricians and craftsmen, between rich and poor. Everywhere leaders appeared in support of the poor: at Liège, Henry of Dinant; at Louvain, Peter Coutereel; in Flanders, Yoens, Ackerman, Artevelde. Generally speaking, after the fourteenth century the craftsmen triumphed, but everywhere only after bloody revolts. Once victorious, the laboring classes in many cities expelled the patricians from all public offices and admitted them only when enlisted in some corporation of craftsmen. In this manner the democratic régime was established in place of the former aristocracy.

Nowhere were those democratic struggles so violent as in Flanders. There the three powerful communes of Ghent, Bruges, and Ypres tyrannized over the smaller cities and the country. In order to crush the supremacy of the patricians, who were the masters in these three cities, Count Guy de Dampierre supported the claims of the craftsmen. In their turn, the patricians appealed for help to the King of France, feudal lord of their count. Thus two parties sprang into existence: the party of the poor, who, faithful to the Count, adopted his banner with the device of the Lion of Flanders, and took the name of

Clauwaerts ("men of the [lion's] claw"); and the party of the wealthy patricians, protected by King Philip, who, owing to the presence of a fleur-de-lis in the royal French banner, were called *Leliaerts* ("men of the lily").

On the cry for help by the latter, King Philip invaded Flanders, defeated the army of the Count, took his vassal prisoner, and treated the country as a conquered land.

But the arrogance of the French and especially of the governor, Jacques de Chatillon, excited the anger of the craftsmen. Those of Bruges secretly recalled the *Clauwaerts* who had been expelled from the city. Under the leadership of a weaver, Peter de Coninck, a revolt was planned. On a summer day of 1302, in the early hours of the morning, the conspirators entered Bruges, surprised the French and their sympathizers, and killed them. This event is spoken of as *Matines brugeoises*, "The Matins of Bruges."

Exasperated, King Philip decided to avenge the revolt and the offense against his authority. A mighty army again invaded the country. Immediately the sons of the Count, John of Namur and William of Gulick, together with Peter de Coninck, organized resistance. The struggle was no longer a merely economic one between patricians and their French protectors on one side and the poor, as partisans of the Count, on the other. It was now a really national struggle, for defeat of the Flemish communes would mean the annexation of Flanders by France.

Under the walls of Courtrai, in the meadows of Groeninghe, the soldier-citizens of Bruges, assisted by many contingents of craftsmen from other parts of the country, met the flower of the French knighthood. The apparently impossible happened. The communes, fighting for the very existence of their country, defeated the army of the most powerful king in Christendom.

That victory is called the "battle of the Golden Spurs," because nearly six hundred golden spurs, belonging to the French knights, were found on the battlefield and suspended, as a token of thanks to God, in the vault of the basilica of Courtrai.

The consequences of the battle of the Golden Spurs cannot be overestimated. From a political point of view it presents the same importance as the battle of Bouvines. It liberated Flanders from French influence and gave the first blow to the hegemony of France in Europe. In Rome, Pope Boniface VIII, a fierce enemy of King Philip, arose in the middle of the night in order to receive and rejoice over the news.

Because the victory saved the national independence of Flanders and practically prevented the political absorption of the other Belgian principalities by Philip the Fair, the Flemings, on July 11 of each year, celebrate the anniversary of the battle of the Golden Spurs as a great event in Belgian history.

The victory of Courtrai gave impetus to real national feeling: all classes, and not least the priests, contributed with all their power to organizing further resistance to the French armies. During the first twenty years of the fourteenth century Flanders, by its own forces, without foreign assistance, resisted the onslaughts of three successive French kings. After the battle of Mons-en-Pevèle (1303), which brought neither victory nor defeat for either side, the Flemings arrived with a new army, and Philip the Fair is quoted as having shouted in despair: "It rains Flemings!"

Finally peace was concluded in 1305 at Athis-sur-Orge. As a result of the intrigues of the French agents and the treachery of the Flemish delegates the conditions were very unfavorable for Flanders. The new count, Robert of Béthune, wanted peace; he did not care for the interests of the cities and the victory of the democratic party. The country was obliged to yield and, in 1319, after a new war, caused by the intrigues of the French King, was forced to abandon Walloon Flanders, including the cities of Lille, Douai, and Béthune. As the county of Artois had already been ceded to France in the time of Philip August, Flanders possessed no more Walloon territory. It retained only the old Germanic portions. It was a severe loss, but by that loss Flanders escaped forever absorption by the French monarchy.

The battle of the Golden Spurs not only had far-reaching results from a national point of view; it also confirmed the victory of the democratic elements over the patricians in Flanders. In those Flemish cities where the latter were masters at the time of the battle they were overthown by the craftsmen after the victory. Moreover, the craftsmen of Liège, in the same year, and under the influence of the defeat of the Flemish patricians at Courtrai, which taught them that they could win if they were organized, inaugurated a revolt against the patricians of their own city. After many years of bloody struggle, they succeeded in wresting from the bishop-prince, Adolf de la Marck, the Peace of Fexhe, that practically founded the liberties of Liège. In Brabant, some years after the battle of Courtrai, in 1306, the craftsmen tried also to imitate their Flemish brethren but here they were severely defeated.

The movement, however, was now everywhere in full swing. The rights of the princes were more and more curtailed by the successful revolts of the craftsmen, and assurances were required that the privileges of the communes would be respected for all time. These demands resulted in the appointment of committees, composed of members of the nobility and members of the cities, the latter preponderating in number, in order to guarantee the privileges granted the commune at its inception and those won during the democratic struggles. We find such a committee in Brabant, where it was called the Council of Cortemberg (1312), and in the principality of Liège, under the name of Tribunal of the XXII.

One of the most famous privileges won by the people during the communal struggles of the fourteenth century is that called the Joyeuse Entrée of Brabant (1354–56). According to the stipulations of that charter of liberty, the territory of the duchy was to remain undivided and undiminished; the seven important cities of Brabant were to keep in their common possession the documents containing the municipal liberties; no offensive war was to be waged, no treaty concluded, no inch of territory ceded, no coin made, without the consent of the subjects. Commerce was to be free, and only legal taxes were to be imposed. The Duke undertook to care for the safety of the roads, to protect his people from arrest in foreign countries, to keep peace between the Rhine and the Meuse, and to respect the treaties concluded with Flanders and Liège. No native of Brabant might prosecute a fellow-countryman before a foreign court. The Duke himself was to be subject to the laws of the duchy.

A comparison of the political situation, as revealed by privileges like these, with the tyranny of the princes in feudal times, brings into a strong light all that was achieved, in point of view of freedom and liberty, by the communes of the thirteenth and fourteenth centuries.

The development of civic freedom and the spirit of democracy, such as we have described, in Flanders, Brabant, and Liège, did not exist, however, in the same measure in all the principalities of Belgium. They were the pride only of those regions where industrial and economic conditions had created the necessary basis for such developments. In the more agricultural regions of the country they were less in evidence or were introduced much later, and they did not make so deep an impression on the life of the people.

Luxemburg, for example, was a very large province, but not thickly populated. It was far removed from the large rivers, while the hills and forests made communication very difficult. In the rocky lines the manors of the robber barons were built, and those watched the passing convoys of merchantmen and attacked them frequently. The historian Froissart depicts very realistically the aspect of the country. Speaking of the passing of the French troops through Luxemburg in 1388, he says:

Two thousand workmen were sent ahead through the forests of Chimay and Neufchateau, in order to clear the way for the troops and to construct a road for the passage of the 1,200 carts of the army. When it had passed the picturesque convent of Orval, the army encountered severe difficulties: it advanced only two miles a day toward Bastogne, through the passes of the Ardennes, infested by savage animals and inhabited only by some colliers. The passage became even more difficult in October, when the rivers overflowed from the rain, when the rocks were slippery, and the roads impassable. The barons of the Ardennes took advantage of it for attacking the convoys and pillaging the train.

In such a country there could be no question of democratic movements, of freedom and the privileges of cities. During the fourteenth century Luxemburg was famous, not for its communes, but for its princes. The most celebrated of them is Duke John, who married Elizabeth of Bohemia and became king of that country. He was the perfect type of mediaeval chivalry. He went through Italy, Poland, France, and Germany as a knight errant, fighting for all good causes. Although he became blind, he assisted at the battle of Crecy (1346) and was killed in the ranks of the French army. His enemy, the Prince of Wales, full of admiration for his chivalrous and heroic behavior, adopted his motto: *Ich dien* ("I serve"), and that motto has remained that of the Prince of Wales to the present day.

The county of Namur was far more receptive of the ideas of liberty and democracy than was Luxemburg. The Meuse and the Sambre flowed through its hills and fields; it possessed commercial roads and copper and iron mines. Here then we find commerce and industry. The craftsmen of Namur won, little by little and but very slowly, a certain share in the government of the cities, and after some serious troubles in 1351 the deans of the craft-guilds were admitted to public office together with the appointees of the Count and the patricians.

There remains the county of Hainaut to be considered. From 1299 Hainaut and Holland, although situated far apart, were united under one dynasty, the family of the D'Avesnes. Holland was mainly inhabited by bur-

gesses and farmers; Hainaut was the last refuge of feudalism. The hills of the Ardennes, extending into the
country, permitted small opportunity for agriculture:
the rocks were crowned by castles, and the forests offered
splendid hunting. There was no trade; the. existing
mines were abandoned. Of course there was the cloth
industry at Mons, Ath, Binche, and Chièvres. But the
weavers did not possess the same spirit of freedom as their
Flemish comrades. A timid attempt at revolt at Valenciennes was quickly repressed. Feudalism continued to
prevail. The knights of Hainaut spent their time in
fighting, especially during the reign of Count William
(1337–45), who organized expeditions against the Prus-
sians and the Moors. At length the noblemen of Hainaut
were nearly all exterminated on the various battlefields
of Europe, and the cities began to add to their importance.
Count Albert of Bavaria, in the middle of the fourteenth
century, favored manufactures, and granted control
over the affairs of the cities to the craftsmen.

On the whole, it was Flanders which played the largest
part in the history of Belgium in the fourteenth century.
The burgesses of Flanders had saved the country from
French domination. But with the foe once defeated,
they began to fight each other, and the main events in
Flemish history at this time are bloody internal struggles
and continuous revolts against the national princes.
Ghent and Bruges, the two most powerful cities of the
county, were continuously in disagreement, and even-
tually took up arms against each other. Since the battle
of the Golden Spurs Bruges had retained its democratic
spirit and Ghent remained, as in the time of Philip the
Fair, the bulwark and the refuge of the patricians. The

craftsmen of Ghent did not succeed in overthrowing their enemies because they were themselves divided. The tyranny of the weavers was often opposed by the other guilds.

It was a question of foreign policy, however, which finally subjected Flanders to a severe trial. In France the dynasty of the Capetians was extinct, and a new family, the Valois, ascended the throne. Edward III, King of England, claimed to have rights to the French crown and decided to inaugurate a war in order to enforce his demands. He sought allies on the Continent and succeeded in obtaining the support of Emperor Louis of Bavaria (1337), to whom he paid a large sum of English gold.

What was to be the attitude of Flanders in the forth-coming conflict? Count Louis of Flanders was a French sympathizer and took the side of King Philip of Valois. The Flemish cities, however, did not desire a rupture with England; their economic interest depended entirely on friendly relations with that country, owing to the fact that they needed English wool for their cloth industry.

At this juncture appeared Jacques Van Artevelde, a man great in Belgian history. He was a member of one of the patrician families, wealthy, and much respected. In 1338 he became captain of the municipal army of Flanders and soon found himself even more powerful than the Count. When the English delegates, sent by Edward III to win Flanders to his cause, arrived in the country, they visited Artevelde as the real leader of public opinion.

Although sympathetic to the English cause, Artevelde, partly fearing the resentment of the French King and partly wishing to prevent his country from becoming the

battlefield of the hostile armies, first tried the policy of
neutrality. He confined himself to assuring England of
his friendship, thinking that this would suffice to win for
Flanders the commercial advantages it needed.

Unfortunately, the conception of neutrality was premature at this moment of Belgian history. The increasing
pressure of Edward III on the one hand and the per-
sistent distrust of France on the other convinced Artevelde that he had to choose between the belligerents.
That was a delicate and dangerous task, for the Flemings
faced a conflict between their commercial interest and
their duty toward their feudal lord, the King of France.
Artevelde, "the wise man of Ghent," acted cleverly.
On his suggestion, Edward III declared himself to be the
true king of France, for he was the grandson of Philip the
Fair through his mother, whereas Philip of Valois was
only the nephew of the former ruler. The Flemings,
easily convinced by these claims, put their scruples aside,
and accepted the idea of the Anglo-Flemish alliance.
The French fleet was destroyed by the English at L'Ecluse
(1340), but Tournai was vainly besieged by the Anglo-
Flemish forces. Artevelde became more and more the
confidant of the English King, who called him "his
fellow" and highly appreciated his shrewd diplomacy.

The power of the "wise man of Ghent" soon aroused
the jealousy of many, and was greatly endangered when
the English King, annoyed by the reluctance of the
Flemings to conclude with him a complete treaty of
alliance, suddenly abandoned his claims and left his allies
in the lurch. A sudden outburst of hostility put an end
to Artevelde's career. His enemies informed the people
that he had favored England too much, that he had given

the treasure of Flanders to the English King, and that he intended to offer the crown to the Prince of Wales. Only the last charge was true. But the people, stirred up by demagogues who had planned the fall of the "wise man," believed what they were told. A furious mob attacked the house of Artevelde. While he was trying to persuade them that he was falsely accused, he was overpowered and ignominiously slain (1345). "The poor exalted him, the wicked killed him," that is the epitaph written by Froissart, his political adversary, in honor of the greatest Fleming of all times.

The assassination of Artevelde was followed a short time after by the death of his enemy, the Count of Flanders himself. Louis of Nevers fell among the French knights on the battlefield of Crecy, where the English King won a decisive victory. The new count, Louis of Male, was an enemy of democracy. He had to meet a serious revolt of the craftsmen of Ghent, under the leadership of Philip, the son of Artevelde. The son of the "wise man" had no particular military or political talents; his extraction alone had commended him to the restless people of Ghent. He tried to renew the alliance with England, but failed. A French army was sent to Flanders in order to assist the Count against his subjects. In the battle of Roose-beke, near Courtrai (1382), the Flemings were defeated and Philip Van Artevelde was killed. The whole of Flanders fell into the hands of the victors, except the commune of Ghent. That mighty city, thanks to the courage of Peter Vanden Bossche and his troops, resisted the kingdom of France for two years.

Finally, Louis of Male, the last of the family of the Dampierre, died in 1384. His death opens the rule of the Burgundian dukes in the history of Flanders.

The many years of internal struggle had seriously injured the prosperity of Flemish trade and industry. The finances of the communes were ruined; poverty was on the increase; the income from licenses had diminished; foreign merchants complained of the insecurity of their goods. Edward III invited many Flemish to emigrate to England, which they did, and the Flemish counts, by punishing the rebellious cities, had themselves cut off many sources of production and wealth. From 1350 on, the German Hansa, whose members resided at Bruges, complained of the heavy taxes, and of the complete lack of peace and safety. In 1380 the Count banished the merchants, charging them with having plotted against his authority and with having assisted the Flemish rebels. This was a serious blow to the prosperity of the country. The Hansa left Bruges for Antwerp. Here began the decline and fall of the once famous seaport.

If we look back at this stage of the political development of the Belgian principalities during the time of the communes we note a growing tendency to consolidation on the part of most of the duchies and counties. At the end of the fourteenth century, Flanders, Brabant, and Limburg were united under one dynasty; the same thing occurred in the case of Hainaut and Holland. Little by little the separation resulting from the treaty of Verdun in the ninth century had disappeared, and all parts of Belgium had gradually experienced the imperceptible drawing together which time had effected. They were ultimately to be united, as a political body, by the dukes of Burgundy. To explain that result is the task of the next chapter.

CHAPTER V

THE UNION OF THE BELGIAN PRINCIPALITIES UNDER THE DUKES OF BURGUNDY

At the very moment when all the Belgian principalities had won their complete political autonomy and rejected the French, the English, and the German influence, they were brought together under the scepter of one dynasty, and became united in a solid monarchic federation. As such, they constitute, between Germany and France, that buffer state represented on the map of Europe by the kingdoms of Belgium and Holland. The unconscious tendency of the preceding centuries was brought to a head in the fifteenth century by the dukes of Burgundy. They were aided in large part by the political circumstances of the time. France was exhausted after the Hundred Years' War and Germany had lost the prestige and the strength of its monarchic power. In favoring the desire for a union of the Belgian principalities, the dukes saved Belgium from conquest or absorption by France. They continued and completed the work of the warriors of the battle of the Golden Spurs. The Scheldt was no longer a political barrier between the east and the west of the country. Belgium, as a united political body, was now for the first time a reality.

The achievements of the Burgundian dukes may be considered from two points of view. We may consider the territorial and geographical consolidation and the political reform.

As for the territorial consolidation, there existed, at the end of the fourteenth century, three ruling houses in Belgium, each of them dominating many provinces, and each hoping to bring the whole country under its scepter. These houses were those of Luxemburg, Bavaria, and Burgundy. The house of Luxemburg had annexed to its hereditary duchy the duchies of Brabant and Limburg; that of Bavaria ruled Hainaut, Holland, and Zeeland; that of Burgundy possessed the duchy of the same name with the counties of Flanders and Artois. It was the Duchess Jeanne of Brabant who turned the scale in favor of Burgundy. Although she had promised the duchy of Brabant to the house of Luxemburg, she gave it to her niece, wife of Philip the Bold, Duke of Burgundy and Count of Flanders. So, in 1404, according to the testamentary devises of the late Jeanne of Brabant, Brabant and Limburg went to Antoine, youngest son of Philip the Bold, while to John without Fear, the eldest son, were given Flanders and Artois. There were thus a Flemish and a Brabantine branch of Burgundy. Antoine, Duke of Brabant, married Elizabeth of Gorlitz, heiress of the duchy of Luxemburg, and annexed that vast territory to his two other duchies (1409). His son John IV, by his marriage with Jacqueline of Bavaria, added to the duchies transmitted by his father the counties of Hainaut, Holland, Zeeland, and the seigneurie of Friesland. John IV was an insignificant prince. History remembers him for having, in 1425, founded the University of Louvain. His brother, Philip de Saint-Pol, died without issue, and thereupon the states of Brabant offered the possessions of the Brabantine branch of Burgundy to the head of the Flemish branch, Philip the Good, Count of Flanders (1430). As Philip the Good had purchased in 1429 the county of Namur, practically all the Belgian principalities came under the same rule. At this moment the unity of Belgium was born. Only the three ecclesiastical principalities of Cambrai, Liège, and Utrecht failed to become united with the other provinces, and in these the Burgundian dukes exerted their influence by appointing members of their family as bishops or by supporting candidates in the episcopal elections who were devoted to their interests.

Philip the Good, whom the historian Juste Lipse called, in the seventeenth century, *conditor Belgii* ("the founder of Belgium"), was known in his own times as the Grand Duke of the West. The fame of his power was carried to the Mediterranean, where his vessels fought the Turkish pirates. He lacked only the title of king. He instituted negotiations with the Emperor for restoring in his favor the former kingdom of Lotharingia. These negotiations did not succeed because he refused to pay to Frederick III, the German Emperor, the sum the latter demanded, and to give the oath of allegiance and vassalage for those parts of his possessions which were fiefs of the Empire. He boasted to an envoy of Louis XI, King of France, that "he wanted them to know he could have been king, if he had only willed it."

His work was nearly destroyed by the extravagant plans and the ambition of his son, Charles the Bold, who succeeded him in 1467. The reign of Charles was dominated by the struggle with the shrewd King of France, Louis XI. This king watched with anxiety the increasing power of one of his vassals, and tried to circumvent his plans in all possible ways. The schemes of Charles the Bold were fantastically extensive, and the historian Philip de Comines said of him: "He tried so many things that he could not live long enough to carry them out, and they were indeed almost impossible enterprises."

As the house of Burgundy tried to dominate the principality of Liège, Charles followed that policy by imposing upon the citizens of Liège the candidacy of Louis of Bourbon as bishop-prince. The people of the principality, stirred up by the French King, rose against the mighty duke. They paid a heavy price. In 1466 the town of Dinant was sacked by the troups of Charles the Bold, and in 1468 Liège shared the same fate. Unspeakable atrocities were committed by the Burgundian army, and fire and sword nearly decimated the populace. These disasters placed the principality for at least ten years under the domination of Charles.

The states of the Burgundian dukes were composed of two sections, separated from each other by independent principalities. In the south, they possessed the duchy of Burgundy and the county of the same name, also called Franche-Comté; in the north, Belgium and a large part of the Dutch provinces were in their hands. From 1469 on, Charles tried patiently but relentlessly to bring together both parts of his state. He took Lorraine by force and got in *engagère* Alsace, Brisgau, and other minor principalities. In the north he succeeded, in 1472, in winning, by the testament of the late Arnold of Gueldre, the duchy of that name and the county of Zutphen.

Adopting the plan which his father had devised, but enlarging it considerably, he began negotiations with the Emperor for the reconstitution of the former mediaeval kingdom of Burgundy, and for his appointment as King of the Romans and successor to the Empire. He failed where Philip the Good had failed.

He intended next to conquer the country of his enemy, Louis XI. After the conquest he planned to divide France between himself and his brother-in-law, Edward of England. In order to avoid the danger, the French King cleverly entangled his vassal in a war with the Swiss. Charles fought the battle of Nancy under very unfavorable circumstances. His army was severely defeated and he himself killed. His body was discovered in the ice of a frozen pool, pierced by three deadly wounds and half devoured by wolves.

His young daughter Mary took on her shoulders the heavy burden entailed upon her as his successor.

The territorial federation of all the Belgian principalities by the Burgundian dukes involved as a consequence the political unification of these provinces. Having but one prince, they also had but one government. It was necessary, of course, that the individual institutions of each principality should disappear, and the political life of the country was subjected to the centralizing tendency of a common monarchy. Above the local institutions were established central institutions, common to all the territories: the council of the duke, an advisory body; the chancellor of Burgundy, a kind of prime minister; the Grand Council, a governmental body, which Charles the Bold, more autocratic than his father, divided into two new colleges, with distinct functions—the Council of State, a political college, and the Parliament of Malines, a supreme court of justice (1473).

Such a centralization of the national institutions was quite necessary if the danger of being dominated by France was to be avoided. France was rapidly becoming united under the leadership of its kings, who possessed a permanent army, the right to impose a perpetual *taille*, and the exercise of sovereign justice. In the face of this united and powerful monarchy, the Burgundian state could not remain separated. The Belgian provinces could no longer remain isolated from each other and limit themselves to an individualistic and egotistic policy. It was seen that everything ought to be concentrated in the hands of a strong prince. That was the new idea that was introduced into the constitution of the Belgian principalities, an idea that had never appeared prior to the fifteenth century. Throughout the Middle Ages the antiquated idea of the state as a collective person distinct from its members never clearly appears. The concept of sovereignty—absolute power subject to no control— was also lacking. The individual life dominated the life of the community. Little by little the renascence of the study of Roman law introduced other concepts, namely, those of state and sovereignty. The students of Roman law, the "legists," stood for a government that would be one, indivisible, strong, absolute, and active. They believed that all that tended to limit the complete exercise of public authority should be discarded: the state was held to be impersonal and almighty. That new concept of the state was embodied in the politics of the Burgundian dukes during the fifteenth century. Centralization and the absolute power of the prince took the place of the former personal and collective privileges. This idea triumphed, not only because the Burgundian dukes were strong, but also because it was in accordance with the needs of the time and the wishes of the majority of the people.

Of course, the dukes, when they tried to realize their political centralization, met with some resistance on the part of the powerful communes. But Philip the Good cleverly avoided any open fight. He simply tried to subject the cities to his control—to prevent them from being a state within the state. He took part in the appointment of the magistrates, ordered their accounts to be examined by his officers, forbade advantage to be taken of the small cities and the peasantry, and made the judgments of their tribunals subject to review by his own councils of justice. Flanders endeavored to evade the results of that policy. There were serious revolts in Bruges (1436–47) and in Ghent (1450–53), and the cities of Brabant, particularly Malines, seemed unwilling to adapt themselves to the new situation.

All this local resistance was ruthlessly broken by Charles the Bold when he became duke. The autonomy of the cities was completely disregarded, the traditions were changed without consideration, the privileges remained unrecognized. Charles kept the appointment of all the municipal charges in his own hands. The omnipotence of the sovereign was, according to him, the only warrant for order and justice, such as he himself desired for his possessions.

Political centralization would, however, never have been achieved by the dukes if they had not enjoyed the support of certain classes of the people. They had, indeed, the help of the noblemen, who were despised and ignored by the communes, and were therefore ready to help all the enemies of the cities. Moreover, the dukes succeeded in destroying the feudal character of the nobility, in softening it, and in converting it into a body of courtiers. They attracted the noblemen by making them royal allowances, by granting them gifts of land or money, offices at court, etc. A golden chain soon bound all the feudalists, once so independent; and life at court soon robbed them of their former spirit of freedom. Before long, the favor of the prince constituted the only chance of success in political and social life. In order to keep the nobles loyal to his person, Philip the Good founded at Bruges, in 1480, the famous and privileged order of the Golden Fleece.

Only the Burgundian and Picardian nobles, however, were to be found at court, occupying the public offices, and entirely submissive to their sovereign. The Belgian nobles could not forget that the rights of the prince, according to national tradition, were not without limits; they desired a guaranty against the dangers of personal government. They desired a government in which the duke would not be able to declare war without the consent of the states, in which he would regulate his expenses in accordance with the income of his domain, and in which he would act only after having taken the advice of his council.

The dukes were also supported in their efforts toward centralization by the clergy. Philip the Good had abolished exemption from taxation till that time enjoyed by the clergy, asserting that the common law was opposed to such privileges. Following the example of the King of France, the Duke limited the temporal power of the clergy, narrowed their jurisdiction, and imposed upon the church his candidates for bishoprics and monasteries. On the other hand, the Duke extended the political power of the clergy, giving them the first place in the States-General and in the councils. The States-General was a new institution, also introduced by the Burgundian dukes. Before the existence of the States-General, the prince was compelled, whenever a levy of taxes was desired, to deliberate separately with the delegates of each Belgian province and to obtain their consent. Philip the Good thought it more expedient to gather them all together in his presence at the same time. That meeting was called the meeting of the States-General. As the States-General did not meet except at the express order of the sovereign, and for his own advantage, this institution served as an instrument for weakening provincial individualism and strengthening the central government.

In the States-General the clergy were granted the first place; they, as well as the nobles, therefore became supporters of the policy of the dukes. By such methods, by persuasion, by distribution of money, and even by violence, the Burgundian dukes succeeded in transforming the institutions of the Belgian principalities into a monarchical rule.

Most of the new institutions were modeled after those existing in France, but adapted to the local situation and needs of Belgium. No principality lost its own autonomy, its own constitution, or its privileges. The Burgundian state was an agglomeration of states, a juxtaposition of territories. There was no universal power; the dukes were not "princes of Belgium" or "princes of the Netherlands"; they ruled every principality separately and were dukes of Brabant, counts of Flanders, dukes of

THE MASTERPIECE OF MATHIEU DE LAYENS: TOWN HALL
OF LOUVAIN

(It escaped destruction during the conflagration of August 26, 1914)

Luxemburg, counts of Hainaut, Namur, etc. But their power was as vast as their wealth. When Philip the Good died in 1467, he left a personal fortune whose annual income nearly equaled that of the republic of Venice and was as much as four times that of the republic of Florence, three times that of the King of Naples, twice that of the Pope and of the Duke of Milan. No wonder that he was called "the Grand Duke of the West."

What about the Belgian civilization in the time of the Burgundian dukes?

We know that, toward the end of the fourteenth century, Flanders suffered a decline after the bloody civil war: the German merchants left Bruges, Ghent lost a part of its population, Ypres was half destroyed, Ostend became a sandy waste. The "polders" were inundated; wolves and wild boars infested the country.

Fifty years later, during the reign of the Burgundian dukes, Belgium had again become the richest country in Europe. That revival was, of course, not attributable to the dukes alone. It must be remembered that the Belgians are an industrious people and that the geographical position of the country is highly favorable. But the political union of all the provinces, peace, and a good administration contributed largely to the revival of the nation. The political work of the Burgundian dukes brought about the unification of coinage, the free relations between the different principalities, the order and safety necessary for the development of trade and industry. From an economic point of view, the dukes endeavored to conserve and to enlarge the resources of the country. They took prohibitive measures against the English cloth industry in favor of the Flemish manufacture. Charles the Bold endeavored to dredge the sand out of the harbor of Bruges and to save that city from disaster. In the fifteenth century Antwerp, supported by the dukes, became the largest market of the north. In Luxemburg the gold and silver mines began to be operated, employing the mine-workers of the region of Liège.

Although the economic policy of the dukes may be described as still somewhat incoherent, it may yet be said to have embraced excellent principles. A declaration is preserved to the effect that "one of the main points of all good policy, upon which the public welfare is based, is to get and to keep good and lasting money, as well golden as silver coin."

Notwithstanding these principles and the various measures taken for the protection of trade, a crisis in the cloth industry was soon apparent. This was due to the transformation in the wool trade. Bruges was the big wool market of the Continent, but, since the development of the English cloth industry, the English producers had kept the raw material at home, thereby diminishing the stock of wool in Flanders. The price had greatly increased, and Flemish manufacturers were obliged to use Spanish wool of inferior quality. This, of course, spelled the decline of the Belgian cloth industry. The decline of Louvain's prosperity was somewhat mitigated by the foundation there of the University in 1425. Nothing, however, could save Ypres. Its craftsmen, threatened with starvation, migrated to England; houses were abandoned and fell into ruin; in 1456 a third of the population was begging for bread along the roads.

Other parts of the country were less affected by the crisis in the cloth industry. Ghent had its grain staple;

Brussels, where the dukes resided, imported articles of luxury; Malines had its Parliament; Antwerp took the place of Bruges as a seaport. Since 1442, English merchants had settled in Antwerp, and this meant the end of Bruges and of the part played by Flanders in the economic life of Belgium. It was now the turn of Brabant. At the same time, a new industry was being introduced into Flanders and Brabant, the technical features of which were much the same as those of the cloth industry. Wool was replaced by flax, and instead of cloth manufacture we hear next of the linen industry. As manufacture on a large scale, mediaeval in its forms and restrictive and exclusive in its spirit of corporation, could no longer support itself, the new linen industry soon came to be carried on in the homes of the operatives, mainly in the country. Driven out of Flanders by circumstances, the cloth industry now sought to prolong its life in a little town of the Ardennes—Verviers, near Liège (1480).

The conditions of trade likewise experienced decline and revival at the same time. In this particular the outstanding feature is the decline of Bruges. As is well known, credit operations on a large scale sometimes bring about big bankruptcies. Until the death of Charles the Bold (1477), Bruges remained the financial and banking center of Europe. It was filled with Italian bankers, among them agents of the Medici, the Portinari, and the Guidetti. A large number of foreign merchants resided at Bruges, grouped in colonies known as "nations." Among them were the "nations" of Florence, of Spain, and of the Osterlings. In 1457 the shipping in the harbor was represented by three vessels from Venice, one from Portugal, two from Spain, six from Scotland, forty-two from Bretagne, twelve from Hamburg, four whale-boats, and thirty-six to forty fishing smacks. The vessels came mainly from Spain and Portugal. They brought merchandise hitherto unknown to the people of Belgium: oranges, lemons, rose-water, candy, jam, oriental tapestry, etc. From the Portuguese warehouses in Africa came monkeys, lions, parrots.

In the course of the fifteenth century, however, for reasons already indicated, the merchants of the German Hansa left Bruges. As a result of the fall of the Flemish cloth industry and the prohibitive measures taken against England in favor of Flanders, the shipping company of the English Merchant Adventurers sent large numbers to settle at Antwerp in 1442–44. They were joined by the Italian, Spanish, and Portuguese merchants. The bankers soon followed. At the end of the fifteenth century the glorious old Flemish city showed 4,000 to 5,000 empty houses. From then on it became known as "Bruges la morte." Its rival, Antwerp, had become the center of the cloth-weaving industry.

The inundations in Zeeland at the beginning of the fifteenth century had considerably enlarged the western Scheldt and afforded a direct route to the sea. Taking advantage of this circumstance, Antwerp, from the very beginning, showed a highly modern and liberal spirit. It reduced the taxes on foreign merchants, whereas Bruges, in order to save the situation, maintained its restrictive and drastic legislation and tried to uphold its economic privileges and its highly protectionist measures. Moreover, Antwerp did not share the revolutionary spirit of the Flemish communes. There were no bloody struggles against the dukes, and there was the best of understanding with the central power.

The new spirit of Antwerp is shown in its commercial organization. There were two fairs yearly, held on the principle of commercial liberty. Those visiting the fairs were protected by a special passport. Whereas a monopoly existed in the professions of broker and money-changer in Bruges, at Antwerp they were open to all. The right of citizenship was easily acquired. In 1460, Antwerp established the first exchange that existed in Europe. At the end of the fifteenth century the city had become the great commercial center of the north. But, as earlier in the case of Bruges, the more important commerce was in the hands of foreigners. The people of Antwerp were but auxiliaries and intermediaries, brokers, forwarding agents, charterers of vessels, etc. The same phenomenon is observable in the Antwerp of today.

On the other hand, the political and economic transformations which resulted in such crises in city life proved advantageous for the peasantry, for the people of the countryside. The decline of the tyranny of the big cities tended to bring to the peasant more and more of freedom. He was now free to engage in industry at home and to become a paid workman in the service of the capitalist. The old restrictions of the feudal law and the law of the manor were gone.

Even in the realm of charity the changing order was manifest. It was now taken in hand by the state. Special ordinances against beggars were issued in 1461 for Flanders and Brabant. Heretofore, the beggar had been abandoned to the tender mercies of the church and of private charity. Thenceforth he was taken in hand by the government. The state refused to encourage beggars; it controlled them and forced them to work. A special license for begging was granted to children under twelve years and to persons over sixty years, and to mothers with numerous children and without work.   Those found begging without a license were imprisoned.   The institutions for charity, heretofore exclusively religious, were taken over by the local governments.   Boards of trustees were appointed by the municipalities and the finances were controlled by the *échevins*.

As for literary and artistic conditions in the Burgundian period, it is to be noted that French influence gradually disappeared after the battle of the Golden Spurs.   French of course remained the language of the court, of the nobility, of the wealthy citizens.   French, together with Latin, also remained as the language of diplomacy.   But it made no more gains.   At this time Flemish began to take its place in civic life.   As a result of the victory of democracy in most of the cities, Flemish became the language of the administration and was used for the registration of real estate and for accounts. Through existing relations with the merchants of the Hansa it became also the language of commercial affairs. Primary schools were established in all the cities, and instruction was given in the language of the people.   The literary works of Van Maerlandt, whose influence has already been described, came freely into the possession of, and were read by, the humblest craftsmen.

When Charles the Bold tried to impose French as the only official language, vigorous discontent was the result, and in 1477 the so-called "Grand Privilege" of Mary of Burgundy resulted in the re-establishment of Flemish. The knowledge of Flemish also spread through the Walloon country.   Walloon merchants settled in Antwerp and Flemish merchants went to Namur and Dinant.

Under these favorable conditions, Flemish literature developed rapidly; but the development mainly affected Brabant. Brabant now took the place formerly occupied by Flanders. The Brabantine dialect, instead of the Flemish one, soon became dominant in literature. One of the best writers of this time was Jan Boendale (†1365), the famous author of the *Brabantsche Yeesten* ("Deeds of Brabant"). Boendale was serious and practical, and had no sympathy for France, like Van Maerlandt. He was an enemy both of the democracy and of the nobility; the merchants and the peasants were the classes with which he showed the most sympathy. Another Flemish author of great fame was Jan Van Ruysbroeck (†1381), also a native of Brabant. He was the herald of mysticism and of divine love, and occupies the first rank among all the religious writers of the Middle Ages. He wrote in a wonderful prose and surpassed everyone in inspiration of thought. The Flemish literature owes also much to another mystic, Gerard de Groote (†1384), of Deventer, founder of the "Brethren of Common Life." The members of that community issued a large number of religious tracts, all of them written in Flemish. They founded excellent schools, where instruction was given by teachers from the University of Paris, and they were the first to introduce the art of printing into the Netherlands. The most famous printer of the Netherlands, Thierry Martens, of Alost, was one of their pupils. Wherever they founded communities and schools they introduced the art of printing, e.g., in Alost, Bruges, Brussels, Deventer, Gouda, Louvain, and Utrecht.

As for French literature in Belgium during the Burgundian period, its output was mainly devoted to the

aristocracy, and consisted chiefly of historical material.
The names of the historians Jean le Bel, Jean Froissart,
Monstrelet, and Chastelain are well known. Froissart was
a cosmopolitan writer, and most of the historians of this
school showed only a dynastic learning. There was no question of patriotism. They praised the Burgundian dukes
because these dukes were their protectors and benefactors.

Artistic life, on the other hand, was not divided into
two separate currents, as was the literary life. In matters
of art, Flemish and Walloon collaborated during the
fifteenth century and together produced a real Belgian
art. The masters of this period were the Flemings Jan
and Hubert Van Eyck and the Walloon Roger de la
Pasture or Van der Weyden.

Since the end of the thirteenth century Belgian art had
become completely original. It was the wealth of city
life that rendered that phenomenon possible. The wealth
of the burgesses served to found many art industries.
Sculpture, painting, and the goldsmith's art were no
longer exclusively religious; they became more and more
secular. The erection of large churches ceased. Painters
were busy decorating guild halls and city halls, banners
and tents, and painting for craft guilds and for dramatic
societies. The oldest products of Belgian art are to be
found in sculpture, especially monuments in stone or
yellow copper. The cleverness of technique and the
realism of outline compel admiration. The artists
copied with exactness what they noted in their sur-
roundings. For the stiff meagerness of the Gothic
style they substituted a more rounded form, and produced a truer art as a result. One of the most
famous sculptors of this period was Claus Sluter, native

of Zeeland, creator of the celebrated sculptures of Dijon. Those masterpieces, made when Ghiberti and Donatello flourished in Italy, enable the Netherlands to share with that country the first place in art of this period.

The painters forsook more slowly than did the sculptors the traditions of the preceding period, but during the period of the Burgundian dukes they made rapid strides. The painters are to be found among the Flemings and the Walloons; they were not influenced by the foreign schools, and they dwelt in the cities of Flanders and Brabant, where the presence of wealthy merchants and the residence of the court afforded them the opportunities for the exercise of their art. Hubert Van Eyck, of Limburg, came to Ghent about 1430; his brother Jan settled in Bruges in 1425; Roger Van der Weyden left Tournai and located in Brussels in 1435. Other famous names are those of Peter Christus, of Brabant; Simon Marmion, of Valenciennes; Juste Van Wassenhove, of Ghent; Hugo Van der Goes, of Ghent; Thierry Bouts, of Haerlem; and the anonymous "Master of Flémalle." This is a period in which art and craftsmanship meant quite different things; the personality of the painter was now in free course of development.

Music also now began to be recognized as the expression of the genius of both Belgian races, although musicians were chiefly found among the Walloons, whereas the painters were mainly Flemings. The names of the musicians Jan Ockeghem (1494–96), a Fleming, and Josquin des Prés (1450), a Walloon, may be mentioned as having substituted the choir with many voices for the choir with one voice, and as having introduced counterpoint in musical composition. Architecture now came to be regarded as of less importance than sculpture. Its tendency was to a profusion of ornaments; the simplicity of lines and the severe majesty of the Gothic style of the thirteenth century disappeared. The prominence of sculptural decoration was especially noticeable in the city halls of Brussels and Louvain (1444–48), the latter the masterpiece of Mathieu de Layens and one of the richest examples of sculpture in the fifteenth century. Louvain was fortunate also in possessing its no less famous university (1425). That seat of learning was founded at the request of Duke John IV of Brabant by Pope Martin V. The faculty of theology was added to the three other faculties (arts, law, and medicine) by Pope Eugen IV in 1432. During the first quarter of the sixteenth century the University of Louvain played an unparalleled part in the intellectual life of Belgium.

Such was the splendid achievement of Belgian culture in the times of the Burgundian dukes. The untimely death of Charles the Bold on the battlefield of Nancy threatened ruin to the marvelous results of their policy. The news of his death was scarcely made public when the strong Burgundian state he dreamed of collapsed. Lorraine, Alsace, and the neighboring countries regained their independence, Liège threw off the yoke, and the shrewd Louis XI, notwithstanding the treaties, annexed the cities of the Somme and of Picardy to France, conquered Artois, and took possession of the duchy of Burgundy and of the Franche-Comté.

This was a disastrous beginning for the young daughter of Charles the Bold, Mary of Burgundy. It was necessary that she be married and so obtain a protector as promptly as possible. The States-General accepted the candidacy of Maximilian of Hapsburg, son of the Emperor Frederick III of Germany. That marriage laid the foundation for the European supremacy of the house of Hapsburg, and gave to Belgium a dynasty which remained in power until the French Revolution.

Prior to the marriage of Mary, the States-General had taken advantage of the disastrous situation in which the young princess found herself, and wrested from her the so-called "Grand Privilege" (February 11, 1477), whereby the Parliament of Malines was abolished and a "Grand Council" was established, with limited power and including representatives of all the Belgian provinces. At the same time, each principality succeeded in obtaining collective provincial privileges. Thus most of the new institutions and rules introduced by the Burgundian dukes were abolished, and the former privileges of the communes were again recognized. After the death of Princess Mary (1482), the reaction of the communes became even more violent. A son named Philip had been born to Mary and Maximilian; history knows him as Philip the Fair. The Belgians immediately recognized the infant archduke, but they continued the fight against his father Maximilian. After a bloody struggle in which both France (assisting Flanders) and Germany (assisting Maximilian) interfered, victory remained in the hands of the Hapsburgs (1492).

The resistance of the Flemish communes to autocracy and centralization was henceforth shattered. Broken and impoverished, they no longer questioned the authority of the prince. Philip the Fair and Charles V continued at peace and achieved the work of monarchic centralization initiated by the Burgundian dukes.

CHAPTER VI

BELGIUM UNDER CHARLES V (1506-55) AND THE BEGINNINGS OF THE HOUSE OF HAPSBURG

Philip the Fair was made duke and count of the different Belgian principalities in 1494. Meanwhile the international situation in Europe had become dangerous for Spain and the Empire. Charles VIII of France had conquered the countries of Milan and Naples. The Hapsburgs and the King of Spain, threatened by the common danger, united against the policy of France and strengthened the coalition by the marriage of Don Juan, heir to the Spanish throne, to the daughter of Maximilian of Hapsburg, and the union of the latter's son, Philip the Fair, with the Spanish infanta, Jeanne. As all the heirs to the Spanish throne died in a short space of time, Jeanne inherited all the rights, and Philip the Fair, sovereign of the Netherlands, became King of Spain.

This event proved of the utmost importance in the history of Belgium. Although regarded as a separate territory, the Netherlands—both Belgium and Holland—became a mere annex of the Spanish branch of the Hapsburg monarchy. For more than two centuries Belgium was ruled from Madrid by sovereigns who were first of all kings of Spain.

This was not yet, however, the case in the time of Charles V, the great emperor of the sixteenth century. Archduke Charles, son of Philip the Fair, known as Charles V at the time of his accession as Emperor in 1519, assumed control of the Netherlands in 1515. The latter included

94

Belgium and Holland, in addition to the county of Artois, and was commonly spoken of as the Seventeen Provinces. The following year (1516) Charles also became King of Spain. His reign was occupied by protracted wars with France, constituting a continuous strife with the powerful sovereign for the hegemony of Europe. In the course of this struggle the Netherlands were continually attacked by Francis I, the French King, and his allies, the Duke of Gueldre, and the La Marcks, Lords of Sedan and Bouillon. The advantage was always with Charles, however, and he was thus enabled to continue the territorial concentration of all the provinces of the Netherlands which was begun by the dukes of Burgundy.

Peacefully or by force, Charles successively annexed East Friesland, Tournai and Tournaisis, the Overyssel, Groninge and Ommelanden, Gueldre and Zutphen to his domains. In the ecclesiastical principalities, which the Burgundian dukes had never been able to annex but only to control, Charles succeeded in winning the temporal power in the bishopric of Utrecht; destroyed Térouanne, the seat of the bishopric of the same name; erected Cambrai and Cambrésis into a duchy in favor of the bishop; and purchased part of the principality of Liège, where he built strong fortresses.

After these achievements, Charles V could call himself the mightiest sovereign in Europe. But a very intricate question yet remained to be settled, namely, what the political relation of the Netherlands should be toward the Empire. The feudal tie between the Empire and the provinces, called into existence while Lotharingia was yet a fief, had never, theoretically at least, been broken; and at the beginning of the sixteenth century Germany still affected to recognize the union (the feudal vassalage) of the provinces with the Empire, in order that they might be the more easily compelled to share in the heavy financial burdens of the latter. The Netherlands, on the other hand, maintained that the union no longer existed. The question was a difficult one for Charles, he being at the same time German Emperor and sovereign of the Netherlands. It took him twenty-five years of negotiations. In 1548, after his victory over the princes of the Protestant League at Schmalkalden, he settled the question by the celebrated Augsburg transaction.

By this provisional arrangement the Empire was divided into "circles." The episcopal duchy of Cambrai, Liège, and the small principality of Stavelot-Malmedy became a part of the so-called circle of Westphalia; the Seventeen Provinces of the Netherlands and the Franche-Comté constituted a new circle, called the "circle of Bourgogne." These states were placed under the armed protection of the Empire, which undertook to defend them as members of the whole. They were recognized, however, as independent and free states, not subject to the laws of the Empire. At the same time, fearing that, through the application of the varying rules of succession existing in each Belgian principality, the union might some day become imperiled, Charles V, by a special act, ordained that the Netherlands or Seventeen Provinces should forever be considered an indivisible whole, in which the first-born son should be regarded as the heir to the throne. In case of deficiency of a male heir, however, the female heir was to be recognized in the succession. This was really a constitutional law sanctioned by the States-General, officially gathered in solemn meeting in Brussels in 1549. The early work of the dukes of Burgundy was now completed and firmly established.

Another task of tremendous importance now engaged the attention of Charles. This was the fight against heresy. The new difficulty presented an entirely novel problem.

When, by the revolt of Luther against the Roman Catholic church, Protestantism began rapidly to spread all over Europe, it quickly found a follower in the Netherlands, whose location facilitated its expansion. In virtue of their historical development, the Netherlands are an essentially Catholic state. Charles V and Philip II, as sovereigns of that state, considered themselves the defenders of orthodoxy, religious unity, and the union of church and state. In opposing what they considered to be a political as well as a religious crime, they invoked the penal laws and criminal institutions as their weapons against what they regarded as a revolutionary movement.

The famous *placarts*, or penal laws, enacted under Charles V to the number of a dozen between 1520 and 1530, were complementary to each other. They were all the work of the government and were approved by the States-General, the prominent members of the military aristocracy, and the knights of the Golden Fleece. They were preventive and repressive at the same time. From a repressive point of view, they distinguished between the crime of heresy and the simple offense against the prescriptions of the *placarts*.

The crime of heresy could be committed only by a man who had been baptized, who from the point of view of the Catholic faith was guilty of error, and who obstinately persisted in that error after having been warned and enlightened. Obstinacy in error was the main point. If there was no obstinacy, but retraction of the error, there was no more crime; there remained only a sin. On the other hand, a simple offense against the *placarts* might be committed by anyone, be he a Catholic, a Jew, or a heretic. Such offenses might be committed, for instance, by *acts*, such as the circulation of heretic books and pamphlets, by sheltering meetings of heretics, etc.

The crime of heresy was to be judged by an ecclesiastical judge, the only one able to discuss those matters. The offense against the *placarts* was to be dealt with by a secular judge, a layman. The jurisdiction of the ecclesiastical judge was limited by strict rules. He might not impose a penalty prescribed by the *placarts*, or any penalty involving the shedding of blood. If the heretic remained obstinate, he was to be expelled from the church and given over to the lay judge, who alone might impose the penalty prescribed by the *placarts*.

The latter penalties were simple and drastic: death by fire, by sword, or by burial alive, and the confiscation of property. The system inaugurated by Charles was anti-judicial and cruel. It was anti-judicial, inasmuch as the penalties were applied both to heretics and to simple offenders against the *placarts*, and thus provided similar punishment for offenses whose intrinsic criminality was wholly different. It must not, however, be forgotten that in the sixteenth century the object of every penal law was to instil terror first of all, and that those guilty of heresy were considered as seditious persons, disturbers of the state, and consequently to be punished by the severe penalties applicable to acts of *lèse-majesté*.

Special officers were appointed for enforcing the *placarts*. These were the so-called "Apostolic Inquisitors" whom Charles V requested the Pope to appoint in 1524. They were only ecclesiastical judges, receiving their instructions directly from the Holy See. Their mission consisted in discovering the heretics, in reconciling them with the church, and in imposing only a canon or ecclesiastical penalty. If the heretic remained obstinate, they were obliged to turn him over to the lay judge. For the first time, in 1546, they received detailed instructions from the Emperor and after that were considered as agents of the state.

Another measure designed to prevent the spread of heresy was the establishment of the new dioceses, but as this was undertaken by Philip II we shall deal with it in another chapter. It remains only to add that throughout the reign of Charles V the system of the *placarts* met with no opposition. The Emperor was a Fleming, he was born at Ghent, he knew his people, and the people accepted from him what they would not accept from his son Philip some years later.

Owing to these circumstances, Charles V was able to complete the work of the Burgundian dukes in another direction, namely, the monarchic centralization of the Belgian provinces. The numerous wars waged by him involved expenses, and, under the rights theretofore granted the country, he was obliged to obtain the consent of the States-General, called together for the purpose, whenever he required the financial assistance of his subjects. In granting the subsidies, the States-General invariably seized on the occasion for exacting some privilege or concession in return. In order to free himself ot this restraint, the Emperor sought to introduce two innovations, which, in France, had practically destroyed the power of the States-General, namely, the permanent impost and the permanent army. To his sister, Mary of Hungary, who in his name governed the Netherlands, he intrusted the proposal of a clever scheme. All the provinces of the Netherlands were to form a defensive union or confederation, in order to be ready to repel the attacks from foreign princes. Should a province be attacked, all the other provinces were immediately to join in assisting it from a military and financial point of view. Such common action would involve the existence of a permanent army and the introduction of a permanent tax.

When the proposal was laid before them, the States-General immediately discovered the trap. Some of them even dared to remark that they did not want to be treated *à la mode de France*. The scheme was unequivocally rejected. The Emperor was obliged to yield. He was far too diplomatic openly and brutally to oppose the privileges of his subjects.

In 1555 he abdicated and went to pass the rest of his life in the Spanish monastery of Saint Just. His son, Philip II of Spain, succeeded him as sovereign of the Netherlands.

CHAPTER VII

PHILIP II AND THE REVOLT OF THE NETHER-
LANDS AGAINST SPANISH RULE (1555–96)

The revolt of the Netherlands against Spain is not merely an event of local Belgian history; it belongs to the political history of Europe. It is an episode of those long and cruel wars of religion which, beginning in Scotland after the constitution of the first Presbyterian Covenant, set aflame the whole of Western Europe. Of course, the occasion for the wars differed in each country, but the cause was the same in every case and the question which was to be supreme in Europe, Catholicism or Protestantism, actuated them all. In this tremendous struggle all questions were finally reduced to one, and as social influences aligned themselves on one side or the other, the tide turned in favor of or against the church. Catholics and Protestants supported their brethren in the faith on the other side of the frontiers. Each side sought a decisive victory; divided influence or co-ordinate recognition was acceptable to neither. Timid persons and politicians seeking to remain neutral were carried away by the current or submerged by it. Neutrality was impossible; everyone was forced to take part in the struggle.

The kings of France, lacking principles and decision, found their own forces divided and were unable to carry out a real international policy. On the other hand, Elizabeth, Queen of England, resolutely ranged herself on the side of international Protestantism, assisting and often directing its attacks. Against her, Philip II of Spain, considering himself as the absolute defender of Catholicism in Europe, set his nationality and his faith. Lacking decision in political matters, he showed no indecision in matters of faith. Against him arose the league of Protestants throughout Europe. They realized that, if he was defeated and his country crushed, the church would be defeated throughout the world. The Protestants therefore concentrated their attack on him in the Netherlands. The geographical position of the latter made interference with England, France, and Germany especially feasible; but they were at the same time the weakest spots in Philip's dominions. Revolt blazed within their borders—such revolt as might result in bringing his power to an end. This Philip realized full well, and determined to go to any limit in order to keep the Netherlands. Nothing was left undone which would serve to suppress every attempt at revolt. This object it was which dictated his unhappy policy in the Netherlands, a policy that resulted in the loss of the northern part, and ultimately in the founding of the separate state of the United Provinces (Holland).

The true meaning of the wars of religion in the Netherlands cannot be properly understood without taking these considerations into account. It will also be useful to consider the characters of those prominently involved in the tragedy, before narrating the details of the tragedy itself.

Philip II, King of Spain and sovereign of the Netherlands, was above all a Spaniard. Educated in Spain, he found himself unable to understand the Belgians as his father had. He did not appreciate their pride, their deep love of liberty, and their respect for the privileges granted them. An autocratic king, he was haughty as only a Spaniard can be. Deeply convinced of the superiority of Catholicism, and possessing principles absolutely rigid in character, he was incapable of compromise —in short, a real bigot. In political affairs he endeavored to arrange every detail himself, and personally to read piles of dispatches by the light of a candle in his dark room in the Escurial. He labored day and night, constantly immersed in thought, and was remarkably slow in reaching a decision. When, however, his mind was finally made up, it was usually too late. Events had progressed in the meantime and when his orders reached the theater of war they could not be carried out, since the situation had entirely changed. That slowness of decision brought him many disasters. Nevertheless, he was an excellent father to his children, and there are extant letters written by him to his daughters, in which it is difficult to recognize the lonely thinker of the Escurial.

He paid a short visit to his subjects in the Netherlands at the beginning of his reign (1557), but left no sympathetic impression behind. His sister, Duchess Margareta of Parma, remained in the country to govern the people during his absence. He was absent to the end. His Flemish subjects never saw him again. From Madrid he directed the affairs of the Belgians, and studied the dispatches which reached him every week.

Margareta, offspring of the amour of Emperor Charles V with the daughter of a Flemish upholsterer from Audenaerde, had been educated for a time in Brussels and had then gone to Italy, where she successively married Alessandro de' Medici and Ottavio Farnese, the latter being Duke of Parma and Piacenza. Although of masculine character, loving sport and exercises, Margareta possessed the feminine characteristics of vanity and shrewdness. She had acquired in Italy a disposition to engage in *combinazione*, and succeeded in playing the game often under very difficult circumstances. Philip of Spain left her as an assistant in her political councils a man of real diplomacy, Cardinal de Granvelle.

Antoine Perrenot de Granvelle, Burgundian in origin, was a loyal servant of his master. He was the man of the *raison d'état*. Philip II never had a more faithful minister. Granvelle desired only the welfare of the King and of the state he represented, and was heroic enough to assume the responsibility for the drastic measures taken by his sovereign. He was a man of real political genius, clear-sighted, absolutely unselfish. The main object of his political plans was that Spain should rule the seas, and it was he who urged Philip II to send the famous *Armada* against England.

When Philip II began his reign in the Netherlands, the financial situation of the government was distressing. Charles V had left heavy debts created by his numerous wars. Public opinion was defiant, influenced as it was by ill will for the unsympathetic King and by the baseless fear that the scheme of erecting new dioceses would be the precursor of the terrible Spanish Inquisition.

The scheme of erecting new dioceses had been conceived by the King in 1559, in order to counteract more strongly the propaganda of Protestantism. The existing mediaeval dioceses were too large to enable the bishops to carry out their mission as guardians of the faith. It was necessary, therefore, that the old dioceses be broken up and divided into smaller ones, so that the bishops would have more opportunity for action in smaller areas. The Pope consented, and permitted the erection of thirteen new dioceses. From an ecclesiastical point of view the country was now divided as follows: the archbishopric of Malines, with the suffragan dioceses, Antwerp, Bois-le-Duc, Ghent, Ypres, Bruges, Ruremonde; the archbishopric of Cambrai, with the suffragans, Arras, Tournai, Namur, Saint-Omer; the archbishopric of Utrecht, with the suffragans, Haerlem, Deventer, Leeuwarden, Middelburg, Groninge. The scheme stirred up violent opposition among the Belgian nobles, the abbots, some of the bishops, and even among the common people. The nobles feared the loss of their political influence through the admission of so many bishops into the States-General, where they would occupy leading positions. Many of the abbots were resentful because their monasteries would be compelled to contribute to the new bishops a part of their income, in support of the new dioceses. Some of the bishops were angered over the division of their former dioceses and the reduction of their spiritual power. The people, influenced by political agents and Protestant propagandists, were led to believe that each new bishop would simply be a representative of the Spanish Inquisition.

The movement of opposition would have been easily repressed by the Belgian nobles had they really been faithful to the King. But, on the whole, they were not. They had the same feelings as the French aristocracy at this time. They were horrified at the idea of the supremacy of the sovereign power. Although not possessing any definite aim, they tried to dominate the Prince and the state by means of the political power they themselves controlled. They were members of the Council of State, governors of the different Belgian provinces, captains in the national army, the famous *bandes d'ordonnance*, and they exercised a tremendous influence on all classes. The political difficulties encountered by the government were for them but favorable opportunities of which to take advantage. The King himself afforded them a chance. With characteristic disregard for the national privileges, he established at Brussels a council called the *Consulta*, an institution of true Spanish type. Composed of a few individuals, it was dominated by the influence of Cardinal de Granvelle, and undertook to decide the most important questions of national policy. The *Consulta* stirred up an opposition of formidable character, guided by the most influential Belgian nobles, the Prince of Orange and the counts of Egmont and Horn. Cardinal de Granvelle became the victim of the most violent attacks. Margareta of Parma first sought to defend him, but, little by little, influenced by the nobles, she finally ranged herself on their side and herself requested the King to recall the unsympathetic minister. Partly through weariness, partly through political miscalculation, Philip II yielded. Granvelle left the Netherlands.

This was a triumph for the opposition. Margareta, who had been moved by jealousy of Granvelle and who had hoped to add materially to her power after his departure, fell more and more under the control of the nobles, who flattered her and took advantage of her feminine vanity. A reign of anarchy and favoritism followed, the friends of the nobles being furnished with offices and perquisites. The political opponents of the King now tried to consolidate and to perpetuate their success. They asked that all affairs be subject to the control of the Council of State, the real national body of which they themselves were the masters; that he should convoke the States-General, and that he should temper the *placarts* against the heretics and abolish the power of the Inquisitors. The granting of the first of these demands would have made the nobles all-powerful in political affairs. From the second measure—the meeting of the States-General—they expected ratification of their conduct and popular support of the opposition they had inaugurated. In dealing with the question of the *placarts*, they played a sort of religious policy calculated to bring them the support of the Lutherans and the Calvinists.

Philip II rejected their demands. Astonished by this resistance, which they did not expect after the capitulation of the King on the question of Granvelle, some of the Belgian nobles, and especially the Prince of Orange, succeeded in embroiling the Protestant sectarians in the struggle. The Calvinists, more warlike than the Lutherans, were more than ready to join the movement, owing to their hatred of the Catholic King of Spain. But, once begun, the movement became an irresistible one. Stirred up by their preachers and assisted by the worst elements of the populace, the Calvinists invaded the churches, smashed the statues of the saints, carried away the treasures, attacked the convents, and killed monks and priests (1566). The Belgian nobles, surprised by the revolt they had so imprudently initiated, were unable to stop it; rather they were submerged by the current.

From this time onward the political anti-Spanish movement became a part of the general movement of the wars of religion. Many Catholics foresaw what would happen and deserted the cause, separating themselves from a revolt that was being directed as much against the church as against Spanish rule.

From the revolt of 1566 and the outrages of the sectarians resulted the later policy of Philip II toward the Netherlands. Hitherto he had but followed the traditional policy of his father, Emperor Charles. He had showed respect for political institutions; he had avoided any cause of rupture. He had tried, of course unwillingly and unskilfully, to satisfy public opinion. His patience brought him nothing but a serious check. He had recalled, in 1561, the Spanish garrisons which had been quartered in Belgium during the war with France; he had sacrificed his loyal minister Granvelle and had capitulated to the nobles. But the more he showed himself to be conciliatory the more audacious became the opposition. This was at first purely political and aimed only at the reconstruction of the Burgundian state as against the Spanish state; later, it had dared to claim liberty of conscience, an unheard-of thing at this period; finally, it had favored the Calvinistic agitation and had caused the desecration of convents and churches.

When the news of this outrage reached the King, he angrily exclaimed: "By the soul of my father, for these crimes they shall pay a heavy price." In the eyes of Philip II, official protector of Catholicism, both the royal and the divine majesty had been insulted, and the claim for autonomy had but aggravated the triumph of heresy His rebellious subjects were to be chastised. He would impose political absolutism upon them as well as the religious control that prevailed in Spain. The iron rule he intended to introduce would preserve for the church and for himself those countries which were the cornerstones of his world-power.

From now on we may speak of the "Spanish rule." The traditionally lax policy of Emperor Charles was gone. The tyranny of Spain was destined to crush the Belgians. That task was intrusted to the Duke of Alva, who came to Belgium as governor in 1567. Don Luis Alvarez de Toledo, Duke of Alva and Marquess of Soria, was a cold and implacable warrior. The greatness of his king was for him the greatness of Spain. He hated the Belgians, who had dared to ask for liberty of conscience, as much as he hated the heretics. He accomplished his terrible mission unwaveringly and remorselessly; his method of government was terror. Accustomed to fight the Moslem Moors of Spain, he knew only two weapons with which to crush the heretics—the sword and the stake. He wrote in one of his letters: "It is infinitely better to keep, by means of war, for God and for the King, an impoverished and even ruined country, than to keep it, without war, undamaged, for the devil and his partisans, the heretics."

Such was the terrible warrior to whom Philip II intrusted a double task: to chastise the rebels and heretics and to subject the nation to the rule of Madrid. Alva arrived in Belgium with a large number of the best Spanish troops. Contrary to all customs in the free Netherlands, they were billeted in the cities. A fortress was ordered built at Antwerp. The counts of Egmont and Horn and the burgomaster of Antwerp were treacherously arrested and imprisoned. But the real leader of the opposition, the Prince of Orange, could not be taken. More clear-sighted than his friends, he had fled to Holland before the coming vengeance. In defiance of all national privi-leges, Alva established an extraordinary tribunal, which the people soon called the "Council of Blood"; that court of justice, established and conducted in a thoroughly revolutionary manner, condemned scores of people who were more or less guilty of revolt against the King. Six thousand victims were sentenced to death and executed. Only political crimes were taken into account, and the condemnation was followed by the confiscation of prop-erty—a remarkably remunerative operation for the Spanish treasure chest. Terror fell upon the Belgians. All who had engaged in the slightest degree in the revolt of 1566 fled to foreign countries; Lutherans and Cal-vinists, panic-stricken, left the Netherlands in large numbers.

Meanwhile the Prince of Orange had sought for help among the German Protestant princes; he gathered an army and invaded Belgium. He had expected a general revolt of the people against Alva at the first news of his campaign. But the soldiers of his army, merely hirelings, and many of them fanatical Protestants, pillaged churches and convents on their way; they disgusted the naturally religious populace of Belgium, and the campaign of William the Silent proved a complete failure. The prince was compelled to seek refuge in France, where he hoped to get help from Coligny and the French Huguenots.

By way of reply to this misadventure of William the Silent came the execution of the counts of Egmont and Horn. The "Council of Blood" charged them with,

ANTWERP

The oldest part of the city, the Scheldt, and the Town Hall

high treason and ordered them to be put to death, on the
Place du Sablon, in the heart of Brussels. Their death
stupified the people and disheartened the nationalists.
Both counts fell victims to the hatred of the terrible duke,
for they were guilty only of weakness and imprudence—
they never really were traitors to their sovereign. The
Belgians always regarded them as martyrs for their
country. Alva now proceeded to introduce into the
Netherlands the features of the Spanish régime, while
his condemnations continued. For the first time since
1561 the new bishops were able to occupy their bishoprics, the Catholic faith was everywhere re-established,
the University of Louvain was visited in order to determine whether it was sufficiently orthodox, the Council of
State was no more called together or given over to Spaniards. In order to secure supplies and money for his
administration and to crush the country economically,
Alva introduced unheard-of taxes, called the *centième,
vingtième, et dixième denier*. This meant a permanent
impost, which the Belgians had always stoutly resisted.
A revolt broke out all over the country. What the
appeals of William the Silent did not effect, the attack
upon the people's privileges and wealth did. The Prince
of Orange cleverly took advantage of it, and, needing the
help of the heretics to fight the enemy, gave the direction
of the movement into the hands of the Calvinists.
Meanwhile a storm of recrimination and complaints,
among which the protests of the bishops and of the
University of Louvain were not the weakest, reached
Philip II. The King understood that he had gone to work
the wrong way, and that the policy of terrorism had not
brought him any real success. He changed his mind and

recalled Alva. The terrible duke left Belgium pursued by the maledictions of the whole people.

His successor, Don Luis de Requesens, was a better man. The change in the King's attitude was immediately revealed by the measures taken by the new governor. Requesens abolished the "Council of Blood," proclaimed a general amnesty, and opened negotiations at Breda with the rebellious provinces. These negotiations failed, however, and the struggle continued on both sides with alternating successes and reverses. Requesens died suddenly in 1575, at a moment when the government was facing an appalling financial crisis. The Council of State immediately took over the regency, till the King should send a new governor.

The Prince of Orange, however, had decided that there should be no peace and that the revolutionary movement should be agitated as much as possible. He had completely gained the confidence of Holland and Zeeland, where he was the real master, and he planned to extend his control over the rest of the Seventeen Provinces. Deeply compromised as he was, any agreement with the King would mean disaster and the end of his plans, which aimed at the separation of the Belgian provinces from the Spanish monarchy. Owing to personal circumstances he had first endeavored to resist Philip II by legal means. During his exile and under the government of Alva he had gone farther and had planned a general revolt, and now that the milder attitude of the King threatened to win back some sympathy in Belgium, especially among the Catholics, he foresaw that only the most daring policy would save the revolutionary movement. Agents were therefore sent to the southern provinces to stir up the people against any attempt at conciliation. As a result of their intrigues, the members of the Council of State were arrested by a furious mob and imprisoned. By the time they were liberated they had fallen completely under the influence of the revolutionary leaders. The States-General were called together by the friendly members of the Council of State, and for nine years exercised the chief power in Belgium. It was during their government, which proved on the whole to be Catholic and loyalist, that the Spanish soldiers, deprived of their pay, arose and sacked the city of Antwerp, killing nearly seven thousand people. This event is known as the "Spanish Fury."

This, of course, gave the anti-Spanish party an excellent chance. Under the pressure of William the Silent, the States-General met at Ghent in 1575, and out of their deliberations was born the famous "Pacification of Ghent." This act was the work of the Prince of Orange, and was intended to reconcile Catholics and Protestants and to settle their religious differences, in order that they might be united in the political struggle against Spain. This attempt at establishing a "peace of religion" was unfortunately premature and provisional. The hostilities between Catholics and Protestants were suspended and religious tolerance was proclaimed; but in Holland and Zeeland, the political sphere of influence of the Prince of Orange, the Catholic worship was provisionally forbidden. The States-General would, it was promised, later on reconsider the whole problem and settle the religious differences definitely. This agreement was, of course, unfavorable to the Catholics, but union was temporarily restored.

Meanwhile Don Juan, the new Spanish governor, had been appointed by Philip II and had arrived in Belgium. Don Juan was the son of Charles V, and the celebrated victor over the Turks in the naval battle of Lepanto (1571). He had no sympathy for the Belgians and did not like the task which was intrusted to him. He attempted, of course, though against his convictions, to negotiate with the rebels, but failed. As we have seen, the Prince of Orange had determined that there should be no peace until his plans had been carried out. By surprising and occupying the fortress of Namur, contrary to the conventions but in order to obtain a stronghold for his protection, Don Juan played, as a matter of fact, into the hands of his enemies. Under the influence of William the Silent the States-General declared the governor a traitor to the country, and called upon Archduke Mathias, brother of Emperor Rodolphe, to be their new governor. Mathias became practically an instrument in the hands of the Prince of Orange, who was appointed as his lieutenant-general.

Now followed a period of anarchy and misrule. Germany, England, and France sent into Belgium a host of sectarians and adventurers; these aided the Calvinists in taking Brussels, Antwerp, and Ghent. Ghent became the center of a Calvinistic republic, where the leaders ruled by terror and began a rigorous persecution of the Catholics. It was now quite clear that the Protestants had gained the upper hand in the struggle and that the national revolt had turned into a war against Catholicism. In the midst of these troubles, Don Juan of Austria died at Bouges, near Namur (1578).

At this very moment, events of great importance took place. The Prince of Orange, contrary to the provisions of the Pacification of Ghent, had again endeavored to introduce a new "peace of religion," which had for its object the introduction of Protestantism into the Belgian provinces other than Holland and Zeeland. The Protestant ministers rejected his proposal. What they wanted was not co-ordinate recognition of Catholicism and Protestantism, but the complete supremacy of their own religion. Seeing that his attempts brought about only discontent of both parties, Catholics and Protestants, William the Silent finally declared himself openly as a Calvinist (1578). His rupture with the Catholics was now complete.

This induced the southern provinces, where Catholicism was still in control, to withdraw their support and to reconcile themselves with the Spanish King. The sole motive of this decision was a religious one. There could be no talk of hostility between the Walloons of the south and the Flemings of the north. This was not a question of racial or linguistic difference. The people of Artois, Hainaut, and French Flanders were disgusted at the excesses committed by the Calvinists of Ghent and the position taken by William the Silent in religious matters. The Catholic spirit of Belgium, imposed on the country ever since the Middle Ages, weighed more strongly in their minds than their national hostility to the Spanish rule. Moreover, two other provinces which joined them —Namur and Luxemburg—had never taken part in the revolt. As we have seen, the province of Brabant, more independent than any other, and, since the four-teenth century, determined in its opposition to foreign interference, had taken the real leadership in the struggle against Spain.

The movement in the south in favor of a reconciliation with Philip II was an essentially popular movement. The nobles of Artois and Hainaut still wavered in their sympathies.[1] The clever policy of the new governor, Alexander Farnese, who succeeded Don Juan of Austria after the death of the latter (1578), overcame their last hesitation.[2]

Alexander Farnese was the son of Margareta of Parma, who had formerly governed the Netherlands. He was of a sympathetic nature, loyal, honest, but firm. He was one of the greatest warriors of his age, but at the same time, being an Italian prince, he distinguished himself as a very shrewd diplomat. At last Philip II had found the right man to govern the Netherlands. Alexander Farnese, highly approved by Cardinal de Granvelle—who at this time resided in Madrid—inaugurated a policy of mildness and conciliation that produced the happiest results. He induced the nobles of the southern provinces, and especially the Count of Lalaing, to abandon their scruples and to return to the service of the King. Both clever diplomacy and gifts and promises of large sums of money played a part in these achievements. From these negotiations resulted the Treaty of Arras (1579), concluded between the representatives of Artois, Hainaut,

[1] According to the unpublished correspondence of Alexander Farnese which I have studied in the state archives of Naples and Parma. See the introduction to the book by A. Cauchie and L. Van der Essen, *Inventaire des archives farnésiennes de Naples* (published by the Royal Commission of History), Brussels, 1910. See also L. Van der Essen, *Les Archives farnésiennes de Parme au point de vue de l'histoire des Pays-Bas catholiques* Brussels, 1913 (Royal Commission of History).

[2] According to the same sources.

Luxemburg, Namur, and French Flanders and the new
governor, as a consequence of which the southern provinces returned to the allegiance of Philip II. A concession made by Farnese was that the foreign troops,
which had for so many years pillaged and ruined the
country, should leave Belgium.

The Treaty of Arras resulted in the reconquest, without bloodshed, of the southern part of Belgium; it provoked a rupture between Catholics and Protestants, the
separation of the Walloons and the Flemings, and crushed
the plans of the Prince of Orange. Henceforth it would
be no longer possible to unite the whole of Belgium against
Spanish rule. William the Silent replied to the Treaty
of Arras by the so-called Union of Utrecht (1579), whereby the northern provinces of the Netherlands united
themselves in the common struggle and decided to carry
on the revolt to ultimate victory. Slowly, but surely,
the secession of Belgium from Holland was in progress.

The Prince of Orange, infuriated by the blow inflicted
on his policy, now proclaimed the forfeiture by Philip II
of the sovereignty of the Netherlands and offered the
crown to the Duke of Anjou, brother of the French King
Henry III (1584). He himself received the title of governor of Holland and Zeeland and remained the real leader
of the union. Philip II replied by declaring the Prince
an outlaw and putting a price on his head. Such an
appeal to murder was common in the sixteenth century
and was even supported by the teaching of many theorists;
today it seems cruel and opposed to every principle of
civilization. A man fanatical enough to fulfil the desire
of the Spanish King was soon found. Balthazar Gérard
treacherously assassinated the Prince of Orange at Delft,

in 1584. So died the leader of the revolt of the Netherlands against Spain. He did not succeed in uniting the whole of Belgium against Philip II, but he initiated the United Provinces of Holland. The Dutch are right, therefore, in calling him the "Father of the Fatherland."

Meanwhile, supported by the Catholic provinces, Alexander Farnese had successively reconquered all the Belgian cities and won an imperishable fame by the siege and conquest of Antwerp. Only Ostend resisted and could not be taken. It seemed now to be the turn of the north, and already the United Provinces were threatened with invasion, when the unwise policy of Philip II suddenly stopped the advance. The lonely autocrat of the Escurial had planned the invasion of England and the conquest of the throne of France, where Henry IV, a Protestant but the legitimate heir, was at war with the Catholic League. To these plans he sacrificed all the resources of Spain from 1587 to 1592 and forced Farnese to suspend his campaign in Flanders, to assist in the transport of troops for the invasion of England, and to aid with his army the League in France. Both enterprises failed utterly, the invasion of England by the defeat of the Spanish Armada, the conquest of the French throne by the final rally of the country to the support of Henry IV.

The obstinacy of Philip II caused the loss of the northern part of the Netherlands, which Farnese would probably have conquered. Alexander Farnese died in 1592 and at his death the Spanish King lost the best governor he had ever had in Belgium. The last years of the sixteenth century were unhappy years for the country. The long and bloody struggle had utterly ruined the land.   The population had been reduced by at least 50 per cent; churches and civic buildings had been burned or severely damaged; trade and industry were in large part gone; Antwerp had lost its commerce, and thousands of people engaged in trade had fled to England, Germany, or Holland.   Artistic and literary activity had come to a complete standstill; and the scientific center of Belgium, the University of Louvain, barely escaped complete ruin.

But Belgium remained Catholic and subject to the Spanish branch of the Hapsburgs, while the United Provinces (of Holland), overwhelmingly Protestant, had in fact become an independent country.   Henceforth Belgium and Holland went each its own way, and their history no longer records common interests, at least until the period of the United Kingdom of the Netherlands (1814).

CHAPTER VIII

THE REIGN OF THE ARCHDUKE ALBERT AND ISABELLA (1598–1633)

Finally, convinced after a long and painful experience that peace was to be restored to Belgium only by new means and other methods than those heretofore employed, and that by waging war he would not be able to win back the northern provinces, Philip II tried another plan. He thought that by giving national sovereigns to the Catholic provinces he might induce the Protestants of Holland to return to their former allegiance and thus restore the lost unity of the Netherlands. In 1598 he decided, shortly before his death, that the Netherlands should be erected into an independent state, whose crown he gave to his daughter Isabella, after she had married Archduke Albert of Austria. If she and her consort should have no children, the Belgian provinces were to return to Spain. This was an important decision, although nobody in Europe believed in the real independence of Belgium. The country was practically under Spanish influence. But autonomy, at least, existed.

Strange to say, the satisfaction felt by the Belgians was at first mingled with some disappointment. As Albert and Isabella were obliged, as sovereigns of "the Netherlands," to continue the war against the northern provinces in order to unite them with those in the south already under their power, the Belgians feared that they would be charged with the heavy burden of war, and this time without the aid of the Spanish finances and of the Spanish army. But Philip II had foreseen the difficulty. He sent the famous general Spinola to their assistance, with an army of excellent Spanish troops.

At first Archduke Albert initiated negotiations with the United Provinces, but his proposals were received with contempt. He was forced to make war. A bloody battle was fought at Nieuport, where the Archduke courageously led his troops against the Dutch under Maurice of Nassau. Although not victorious, Albert decided to besiege Ostend, the only Belgian city left in the hands of the rebels. The siege of Ostend lasted three years, from 1601 to 1604. On both sides deeds of heroism were numerous. Three rings of fortifications had to be taken and every trench was stormed at the cost of many lives. At length Ostend, continuously battered by artillery, could no longer resist the energetic assaults of the soldiers of Spinola. It surrendered, but only its ruins were left in the hands of the victor.

After the fall of Ostend, the Archduke, wishing to put an end to this war of exhaustion, again opened negotiations with the United Provinces, and succeeded in concluding a truce for twelve years (1609–21). During that time Albert and Isabella did their best to heal the wounds of their people. Their reign was one of peace and of reconstruction. The sovereign power was even stronger than before the crisis of the sixteenth century. No revolt troubled the happy years of the Archduke's rule. National institutions were not disturbed, the re-establishment of order was attempted by law rather than by force. In 1611 a meeting of magistrates and lawyers was called in order to codify the judicial provisions and to inaugurate a reform of civil and criminal law. The fruit of that attempt was the *Édit perpétuel*, a judicial monument of great importance. At the same time the old customs, the unwritten law of the Belgian principalities and cities, were reduced to writing and published in definite form by order of the sovereign.

In addition to the respect they manifested for the customs of the country, Albert and Isabella showed the utmost interest in the restoration of every kind of social activity. Zealous for the welfare of Catholicism, they undertook to restore the religious life of the country. Three hundred churches and convents were rebuilt or founded. The religious orders of the Jesuits, the Carmelites, etc., found in the sovereigns hearty and generous protectors. The lost treasures of the churches had to be replaced, and the restoration of worship brought about the revival of the goldsmith's art and of painting. The Flemish school of painting again became as famous as in the time of the Burgundian dukes. The head of this school was Peter Paul Rubens; and among his pupils he counted artists like Van Dyck, Teniers, and Jordaens. Public education was encouraged and many colleges and academies were opened for the teaching of Greek and Latin. The University of Louvain was accorded special protection. In 1607 Drusius, abbot of the abbey of Parc, near Louvain, and Van Craesbeke, councilor of Brabant, were appointed to inspect the University. Another delegate, the Nuncio Caraffa, was sent by the Pope. The system of "visitation," as it was called, lasted, with interruptions, till 1617, when a complete scheme of regulations was enacted. The jurisdiction of the academic authorities, the privileges of the University, the interests of teaching and of the various colleges, the rights and duties of professors, the granting of degrees, the discipline and conduct of the students—everything was carefully dealt with. The visitation of 1617 established the authority of the University of Louvain and gave it a legal status.

The excellent results of the new rules were immediately apparent. At this time seven or eight thousand students, among them Dutchmen, Frisians, Flemings, Germans, Frenchmen, Spaniards, and Italians, were in attendance at the University. The faculty of law became especially notable, and professors such as Peckius, Coursèle, Tulden, Perez, and Gudelin were regarded as eminent authorities. In letters the humanists Justus Lipsius and Erycius Puteanus, Valerius Andreas and Nicholas Vernuleus were famous. Albert and Isabella showed clearly their lively interest in the institution by attending one of the lectures of Justus Lipsius.

Although artistic, literary, and scientific interests flourished during the reign of Albert and Isabella, the trade and industry of Belgium enjoyed no such revival. Antwerp was closed and had no access to the sea, as the Dutch blocked the Scheldt, and all commerce with the colonies of the New World was forbidden to the people of Belgium by Spain. Moreover, the peace and safety necessary to the development of trade were continually threatened by France in the south and by the United Provinces in the north.

The private life of Albert and Isabelle was modest and simple. Their court at Brussels was an example of morality and seriousness, although they were not given over to bigotry. Isabella was a cheerful princess; she liked to mingle sometimes with the people and to take part in their rejoicings and their sports.   Both sovereigns were very popular.

Sorrow filled the souls of the Belgians when the Archduke died in 1621, without issue.   According to the testament of Philip II, Belgium was held obliged to return to Spanish rule.   Indeed, Spain immediately took possession of the country and, although Isabella remained at Brussels, she was no longer a sovereign, but a simple regent in the name of the King.   When she died in 1633, the universal mourning in town and country proved how well she had succeeded in winning the sympathy of the Belgians.[1]

[1] Attention has been called to the fact that the present King and Queen of the Belgians bear the same names: Albert and Elisabeth (Isabella).

CHAPTER IX

THE LAST YEARS OF THE SPANISH RULE (1633–1715)

The last eighty years of the seventeenth century were an unhappy period for Belgium. France, under Richelieu and Louis XIV, continually attacked the declining Spanish monarchy, and sought to wrest from it the Belgian provinces piece by piece. From 1622 to 1648 France was assisted in this policy of conquest by the United Provinces of Holland. Each treaty of this period marks a territorial diminution of Belgium and sometimes likewise a decisive blow at the elements of its material prosperity. The Treaty of Munster, concluded in 1648 between Spain and the United Provinces, remorselessly sacrificed the commercial interests of Belgium. According to this treaty it was agreed that the Dutch should have the right to control and to close the Scheldt, the very source of Antwerp's wealth. It was also agreed that henceforth the United Provinces should definitely retain their independence, won by William the Silent and his sons, should even remain in possession of Northern Brabant and Northern Flanders, and should divide with Belgium the sovereignty over Maestricht.

The act which established the final separation between Belgium and Holland constituted also the first act of hostility of the latter. As a consequence of the Treaty of Munster, Limburg was divided between both countries in 1661. The Dutch obtained the larger part of the country of Fauquemont and Daelhem and a portion of Rolduc.

Other territorial losses were forced upon Belgium some years later. In 1659, France acquired nearly all the country of Artois, by the Treaty of the Pyrennees; in 1668, French Flanders and Tournaisis, by the Treaty of Aix-la-Chapelle; in 1678, Franche-Comté, Cambrai and Cambrésis, and the rest of Artois, by the Treaty of Nimègue. On the whole, the defeats suffered by the Spanish monarchy at the period of its decline cost Belgium, hopelessly attached to the dying body, the north of Flanders, and the south of Flanders, of Hainaut, and of Luxemburg.

Each treaty terminated a war; and from the numerous negotiations already mentioned it is not difficult to realize how many wars Belgium was forced to endure on her own soil. Dutch, French, English, Spanish, Germans, successively trampled over the rich fields of Flanders and the industrious country of the Walloons. In fifty years, from 1642 to 1709, no less than ten famous battles were fought on Belgian soil. Belgium was already at that time "the cockpit of Christendom," a designation found in an old English book, *Instructions for Forreine Travell*, written in 1642 by James Howell, a clerk in the diplomatic service.[1] Howell says:

. . . . For the Netherlands have been for many years, as one may say, the very cockpit of Christendom, the school of arms and rendezvous of all adventurous spirits and cadets; which makes most nations beholden to them for soldiers. Therefore the history of the Belgic wars are very worth the reading; for I know none fuller of stratagems, of reaches of policy, ... nor a war which hath produced such deplorable effects, directly or collaterally, all Christendom over, both by sea and land.

---

[1] This information is given by Ensor, *Belgium*, pp. 103–4. At about the same time, the Nuncio Bentivoglio, in his famous *Della Guerra di Fiandra*, calls Belgium the *arena militare* of Europe.

COURT-YARD OF THE PALACE OF THE BISHOP PRINCES IN LIÉGE

What all these wars meant for the poor inhabitants of the country may be imagined when the devastation wrought by huge armies in Poland today is borne in mind. And it must be remembered that the armies of the belligerent powers in the seventeenth century were, to a large extent, composed of mercenaries without any feeling of patriotism, without discipline, without morals, who saw in military occupation only an opportunity for excesses and outrages of all kinds, who revolted when not regularly paid, and who pillaged the friendly country they were hired to defend as well as the enemy's territory. Massacre, burning, looting, awful tortures inflicted on the unhappy inhabitants in order to force them to reveal the spot where their money was kept—all this was daily work for those rough hirelings. In the village of Meix-devant-Virton, in 1636, the whole populace was burned alive in the church where it had taken refuge, not by the enemy, but by the Spanish troops intrusted with their defense.[1] Ruin, disease, and poverty were the terrible lot of Belgium during this sinister century.

What of the internal situation of the country? After the death of Archduke Albert (1621), the Spaniards increasingly dominated the destinies of Belgium. A Spanish army, paid by Spain and under a Spanish commander, permanently occupied many fortresses and important cities. Those members of the Belgian aristocracy who sought to obtain influence with the intruders found themselves compelled to marry their daughters to Spaniards. The Spanish government put the native nobles entirely aside, and all important matters were discussed in *Juntas*—special committees composed of Spaniards.

[1] Mentioned by G. Kurth, *Manuel d'histoire de Belgique*, 2d ed.

This unhappy state of things in 1622–33 provoked the so-called "conspiracy of the Belgian nobility against Spain." This was the work of some prominent *seigneurs* who failed to realize the historical conditions and the times in which they lived. They fondly believed that, with the help of France and of the United Provinces, they could start another Belgian revolt, like that of the sixteenth century, and that they could obtain support from the army and the people. They found themselves seriously mistaken. The Belgians, wearied of their misfortunes, refused to follow them. They had no confidence in the movement. The attempt failed and the conspirators were obliged to flee to foreign countries to avoid criminal prosecution. As for the States-General, except in 1600 and 1632–34, they were never called together; only when there was talk of peace negotiations with the United Provinces were they allowed to meet.

The rule of the Hapsburg dynasty in Spain came to an end with the death of the last heir, Charles II, in 1700. The latter had provided in his will that Philip of Bourbon, grandson of Louis XIV, of France, should be his successor and consequently sovereign of the Netherlands. As a matter of fact, it was Louis XIV who governed in the name of Philip. The absolutist system which existed in France was suddenly introduced in Belgium, and organized by the Count of Bergeyck, with the help of French generals. This régime did not last long; in 1702 the War of the Spanish Succession broke out, in the course of which England and the United Provinces concluded an alliance against Louis XIV.

Three treaties terminated the struggle—that of Utrecht, that of Rastadt, and that of Bade (1713–14).

The contracting powers decided that the Netherlands—
that is to say, Belgium—should be transferred to the Austrian branch of the Hapsburgs.   They would serve as a
barrier for the protection of the United Provinces against
any menace from France, and it was determined, therefore, that the Dutch should continue to occupy Belgian
territory provisionally till all questions had been settled.
A final agreement was reached by the Treaty of Antwerp,
better known as the "Treaty of the Barriers" (1715),
somewhat modified by the Hague Convention of 1718.
These several conventions placed the Hapsburgs of Austria
in full possession of Belgium.

CHAPTER X

BELGIUM UNDER THE HOUSE OF AUSTRIA
(1713–89)

When the house of Austria came into possession of Belgium only ten provinces out of the seventeen of the old Spanish Netherlands were left: Brabant, Limburg, Luxemburg, Namur, Hainaut, the seigniory of Tournai, the seigniory of Tournaisis, Flanders, the seigniory of Malines, a part of Gueldre. West Flanders, including Ypres and some adjoining districts, formed a separate department.

The Hapsburgs of Austria were not to be regarded as foreign conquerors of Belgium. From the outset they had claimed to be the natural heirs of the Hapsburgs of Spain, and that claim was admitted by France, England, and Holland, and by the States-General of the Belgian provinces. There could be no question of Austrian "domination." In their relation to Belgium the Hapsburgs assumed the title of natural prince, as did Charles V at the beginning of the sixteenth century. Moreover, by the Treaty of the Barriers, Charles VI of Austria publicly proclaimed that his house assumed the rule over Belgium, subject to all the restrictions and guaranties to which the Hapsburgs of Spain had been subject. According to the treaties, Belgium was ceded to the Austrian Hapsburgs on condition that the predominance of the Catholic church in the country as well as the rights of the states and cities be recognized. The Catholic church and its position as the religion of the state were to be respected on account of the desire of France to erect a moral and religious barrier between herself and Protestant Holland; the popular rights were to be respected because the theory of the European balance of power required that the Emperor should be permitted only a limited sway. A strong, universal monarchy was no longer possible in Europe.

The theory of the European balance of power had found expression through the Treaty of Westphalia (1648), whereby Europe ceased to be exclusively and officially Catholic, and Protestantism was granted recognition in law. Since the arbitration of the Pope in international matters was no longer possible, owing to the refusal of the Protestant powers to acknowledge his decisions, each country had to rely only upon itself. The weaker states had only one protection, therefore, namely, to unite against any power which might try to absorb them. Out of these principles grew the idea of the European balance of power, according to which no state was to be allowed to grow strong enough to menace the peace of the world.

The external constitution of Belgium under Austrian rule having been established, Charles VI proceeded to protect the rights of his family in respect to internal conditions. As Charles V had established the principle of the indivisibility of the Spanish Netherlands by the Augsburg transaction, already mentioned, the new Emperor established the same principle for the "Austrian Netherlands" by a similar act, the "Pragmatic Sanction" of 1725. Belgium was forever to be kept as an indivisible whole, the eldest son to be heir to the throne, and the right of succession of the female descendants in case of the failure of a male heir was again admitted.

Well-defined obligations to the United Provinces of Holland were imposed upon Belgium by the Treaty of the Barriers. The Belgian sovereign was required to permit the presence of Dutch garrisons on Belgian soil, as a protection for Holland against France, in the cities and fortresses of Namur, Tournai, Furnes, Warneton, Ypres, and Knocke. A heavy yearly subsidy was to be paid by Belgium for the maintenance of those garrisons. The sovereign was also required to recognize the closing of the Scheldt, imposed by the Treaty of Munster (1648). Holland even claimed the right to prevent the Belgians from trading with the Indies.

Notwithstanding these claims, Charles VI had tried to restore Belgian trade by the foundation of a shipping company, the "Compagnie d'Ostende," created under an imperial charter, for commercial dealings with America. But the opposition offered by Holland, supported by France and England, so influenced the weak Emperor as to induce him to suspend and finally to disband the company—the only hope for the restoration of national trade.

The obligation to maintain foreign garrisons in Belgium was both drastic and humiliating. Empress Maria Theresa, who succeeded to Charles VI as sovereign of the Austrian Netherlands in virtue of the provision of the "Pragmatic Sanction," tried to avoid the obligation of the "Barrier" by withholding payment due to the foreign garrisons. The final blow to this unjust system was given by her son, Emperor Joseph II, who simply ordered the demolition of the fortresses still occupied by the Dutch on Belgian soil.

Joseph II, who was greatly interested in the restoration of the prosperity of the country, even attempted to secure

teachings of Febronianism.   An absolutist by conviction,
an enemy of the liberties of the church, despising all
things of the past, and lacking in the adroitness which
characterized Maria Theresa's government, he sought to
put in force without delay the new concept of human
society that he had conceived.   He tried to force upon
Belgium a whole series of reforms, by means of sovereign
decrees, between the years 1781 and 1787.   The fundamental ideas at the basis of these reforms may be sum-
marized as follows: the secularization of political society;
the incorporation of the Catholic church in Belgium as a
part of the national Austrian church;   and the recognition
of the sovereign power as absolute and unlimited.

The political secularization of Belgium was attempted
by the Edicts of Tolerance, issued in 1781–82.   The
ecclesiastical jurisdiction was suppressed;   non-Catholics
were put upon nearly the same level as Catholics, and
public worship was permitted to them under certain
restrictions.   Subject to a dispensation from the sovereign, they were admitted to public offices and could
become burgesses and members of craft-guilds.   In 1784
another edict fixed new rules for marriages, and prevented
the ecclesiastical judge from dealing with the canonical
impediments declared by canon law.

As for the subordination of the church to the state, the
religious orders were no longer allowed to show obedience
to their foreign superiors;   the jurisdiction of the Nuncio
of Cologne over Belgium was abolished;   the Belgian
bishops were forbidden to correspond with Rome on the
matter of dispensations for marriages;   a large number of
convents were declared to be useless and were suppressed,
their properties being placed under the administration of

the state; parishes were delimited by the government; all the confraternities of a religious nature were suppressed and replaced by a single one, which the Emperor-Philosopher called the "Brotherhood of Love for Fellow-Creatures." All the seminaries for the education of priests were closed, and in 1786 a General Seminary was established at Louvain and in Luxemburg, at which theology was to be taught, subject to the control of the state. A very drastic measure was the suppression of any subsidy to the society of the Bollandists, the Belgian Jesuits who were responsible for the criticism and the publication of the Lives of the Saints, and who were known all over Europe for their scientific methods and their superior culture.

In 1787 came the upheaval of the political institutions. The three "collateral councils"—the Council of State, the Privy Council, and the Council of Finances—were abolished. The Secretary of State, the provincial states, the provincial councils of justice, the seigniorial or manorial justice, the jurisdiction of the *échevinage*, the ecclesiastical tribunals, the special tribunal of the University of Louvain which had jurisdiction over offenses committed by students, and all other courts of justice except the military tribunals, were at one stroke suppressed. Joseph II, by a simple act of his sovereign will, wiped out the old institutions and introduced the Austrian autocracy.

But the Belgians, who had always fought against the enemies of their institutions and privileges, did not submit peacefully to this brutal attack upon their liberties. Of course, many of the reforms of the Emperor were not open to criticism, and his motives cannot be said to have been wholly wrong. His efforts, however, were too general in their nature, and were attended with too far-reaching results. At first there was only passive resistance. The bishops had begun by protesting against the religious reforms. The general edicts of 1787 called forth a storm of revolt among all classes of the people. Declarations, petitions, manifestos poured in upon the Emperor's court. The edicts of 1787 were thereupon partly suspended. But the religious reforms were not abated. The establishment of the General Seminary and the order for the closing of the diocesan seminaries were not rescinded, and force was resorted to against the Archbishop of Malines, Frankenberg, and the University of Louvain in carrying them out. This shocked the Belgian people, who at heart were Catholic, and the harsh measures of the Austrian General D'Alton made the situation still more critical. Two parties came into existence: that of the nationalists, called "Patriots," and that of the Austrian sympathizers, called by the people "Figs." In 1788, owing to the resistance of the states of Brabant and Hainaut, the arrest of their members and the abolition of the privileges of Brabant, among them the famous "Joyeuse Entrée," were ordered. General D'Alton became more and more dictatorial and cruel. The result was a serious revolution, known in history as the Brabantine Revolution (1789).

The revolt was the consequence of two elements among the people, which though at heart directly opposed to each other were temporarily united against the foreign tyranny. Each movement had its own leader, Van der Noot and Vonck, and both were lawyers of Brabant. Van der Noot proposed to deliver Belgium by the assistance of foreign powers, especially Prussia—the enemy of Austria—and

Holland. Vonck, on the other hand, placed his confidence in the Belgians alone, and told the people that the great powers would betray them. Both were forced to flee the country in order to escape the anger of General D'Alton. Both established committees for revolutionary propaganda, Van der Noot in Holland, where he established connections in Prussia; Vonck in the territory of the principality of Liège. Later both committees succeeded in agreeing upon a common plan of action. Like William the Silent in the sixteenth century, Van der Noot issued a manifesto proclaiming the deposition of Joseph II as sovereign of the Austrian Netherlands. A national army, recruited on foreign soil, invaded Belgium. The Austrians were defeated and compelled to evacuate the country, except Luxemburg, where they made a stand. The victors then proclaimed a republic, known in history under the official title of the "République des États Belgiques unis" (Republic of the United States of Belgium). In each province the body of the states—delegates of the clergy, the nobility, and the people—were given the exercise of sovereignty, and the traditional institutions of the Burgundian times were restored. In 1790 the provinces held a general meeting at Brussels, where the federal pact between them and the central power was established by the so-called Act of Union.

According to this act, the provinces of the Catholic Netherlands constituted themselves a confederation, under that name. The confederation exercised sovereign power, and controlled the common defense, the power of making war and peace, the recruiting and maintaining of a national army, the making of alliances, the coinage of a common currency. The power residing in the confeder-

THE TOWN HALL OF BRUSSELS AND THE GREAT SQUARE

ation was exercised by a Congress composed of deputies from all the provinces, who acted without referring back to the provincial states. Each province had a certain number of votes in the Congress: Brabant 20 votes, Flanders 22, etc. The confederated provinces made a declaration favoring the Roman Catholic faith and the maintenance of relations with the church as before the reforms of Joseph II. Each province retained its autonomy and sovereign rights, and all powers not delegated to the Congress. In case of attack all provinces were to join in the defense of the one attacked. This, we know, had been the dream of Emperor Charles V in the sixteenth century. The great ruler must have rejoiced in his grave! The Congress was presided over by a president, who held office for a limited period, and three committees were created within the Congress: one for political, one for military, and one for financial affairs. The president was assisted by a prime minister and a secretary of state.

It is hardly necessary to call attention to the fact that there is a very close resemblance between the constitution of the Belgian Republic and the first constitution of the American Republic, whose articles were approved in 1777. The question whether the Belgian Patriots were in any way inspired by the first American constitution remains unsettled, as it has not yet been studied in this light.

Alas! the "République des États Belgiques unis" did not live long. Internal struggles between partisans of Vonck, who fell more and more under the influence of the French revolutionary clubs and talked much about national assemblies and popular sovereignty, and the partisans of the more conservative Van der Noot paved the way for the final collapse. But the bitterest disappointment came from outside. The great powers—England, Holland, and Prussia—which had liberally encouraged the Patriots in their revolt because of its tendency to weaken Austria and to prevent her policy of extension in the east of Europe toward Constantinople, betrayed the young republic. Their support of the Belgian claims had been inspired by the idea of the European balance of power, but they cared little for the independence of the country. The conference held at Reichenbach, in which England, Prussia, Holland, and Austria participated merely resulted in a decision to restore Austrian rule in Belgium, with guaranties for the maintenance of the ancient institutions and an amnesty for the past. The Treaty of the Hague (1790) definitely settled the question. Thus died the Belgian republic after a year of existence, but it had not existed in vain. The Treaty of the Hague gave constitutional value to facts and principles which hitherto had depended only on the good will of the sovereign. Emperor Leopold II again occupied the "Austrian Netherlands"; but the new Austrian rule was to have as short an existence as had the Belgian republic. The French Revolution was destined to drive the Austrians out of Belgium.

CHAPTER XI

BELGIUM UNDER FRENCH DOMINATION
(1792–1814)

The French revolutionary clubs had exerted a powerful influence on Vonck. The effect of their teachings had also been felt in the independent principality of Liège and had provoked a rising of the people against the bishop-prince. But the revolt of Liège, which occurred at the same time as the revolt in Belgium against Joseph II (1789), was quickly suppressed.

When France itself fell a victim to the revolutionary leaders, the great Revolution broke loose. The French soon found themselves confronted by a European coalition and were forced into war. Since Austria was inimical to the Revolution, the French troops invaded the Belgian possessions of the Hapsburgs in 1792 under the leadership of General Dumouriez. They found not a few sympathizers in the country. The partisans of Van der Noot looked to the French to deliver them from the Austrian yoke; the partisans of Vonck had always been agents of the French revolutionary leaders, and desired the annexation of their country to France. After the victory of Jemappes (1792), the French entered Belgium, loudly proclaiming that they came as liberators of the people and desired only the destruction of Austrian tyranny. Although the excesses of their troops seemed to contradict this statement, the people believed them. Then came the second and final defeat of the Austrians at the battle of Fleurus (1794). Both Belgium and the principality of Liège were occupied by the victors.

A period of terrible excesses followed. The French National Convention entirely abolished all the ancient institutions; a provisional administration was established, and "clubs" with political aims were introduced into all the cities. Taxes, requisitions, systematic pillage, outrages on religious convictions rained upon the unhappy inhabitants. General elections were forced upon the Belgians and manipulated by the "Sans-culottes" and political agents so as to give the impression of a referendum, through which the people should express their desire to be annexed to France. This plan encountered general hostility throughout the country. Thereupon the National Convention, by a law voted and applied on October 1, 1795, simply annexed Belgium and the principality of Liège. As Austria was too weak to defend her possessions, it formally ceded the Austrian Netherlands to France and recognized the annexation by the Treaty of Campo Formio (1797).

The French now treated the conquered territory with great harshness. The followers of the Catholic religion were severely persecuted, the churches were closed, the priests were sentenced to death or deported to French Guiana and to the islands of Ré and Oléron, the Catholic worship was suppressed and replaced by that of the "Goddess of Reason." For the first time in Belgian history military conscription was forced upon the inhabitants, and the youth of the country was compelled to shed its blood on foreign battlefields for a régime it abhorred.

This naturally stirred up bitter resentment; and, even as they had risen against Joseph II, so a part at least of the Belgians rose against the French. This revolt is known as the War of the Peasants (1798–99), because it was mainly the people of the countryside in Flanders, Campine, and Luxemburg who fought in defense of their hearths and their religion. They fought heroically with old weapons, scythes, pikes, and guns of old pattern, under the leadership of a few nobles and burgesses. There is a close resemblance between their struggle and that of the French peasants in the Vendée. But what could they accomplish against the well-equipped armies of the Republic? The egotism of the educated classes, which gave them no support at all, and their lack of training and experience, soon brought their valiant resistance to an inglorious end. One after another their bands were exterminated, and those who did not fall on the battlefield died against a wall by the bullets of a firing squad.

Their gallantry did not save the country. Belgium remained fifteen years longer under French domination. The Concordat concluded in 1801 between Pope Pius VII and Napoleon Bonaparte brought the religious persecution to an end, and the Catholic worship was restored. When Bonaparte had become Emperor Napoleon I, the glory which surrounded his name made a profound impression on the Belgians, and the great Emperor became very popular among them. Antwerp attracted all his attention; and it is due to him that the Scheldt, after a century and a half of being closed, was again opened to trade and was freed from the tyrannous control of the Dutch. As military conscription still prevailed, the Belgians filled the ranks of the imperial army, and their blood was shed for the fame and the power of Napoleon all over Europe. The conqueror left on the country, however, the impress of his spirit of organization in the famous *Code Napoléon*, that monument of civil law that still forms the basis of Belgian jurisprudence. The spell of his name appeared from the fact that after the defeat of his armies at Leipzig in 1813 there was no revolt against him in Belgium as there was in Holland.

The fall of Napoleon ended the French domination of the Belgians (1814). However, the diplomats who rearranged the map of Europe, while the once mighty Emperor was sent to St. Helena, had determined that the country was not to be restored to its former political status.

CHAPTER XII

THE DUTCH RULE AND THE BELGIAN REVOLT
OF 1830

After the fall of Napoleon, the powers were called upon to decide the political status of Belgium. The Belgians were not consulted in the matter, vitally important as it was, and their country was considered merely as the spoil of the Allies. The main idea that actuated the Congress of Vienna (1814–15) in rearranging the map of Europe was to prevent a new menace from the side of France. This country was not allowed to hold more territory than it possessed in 1789, before the outbreak of the Revolution; at the same time the Allies who had defeated Napoleon sought to erect a bulwark against any new extension of France in the North. They could have granted independence to Belgium, but as the country was weak it seemed that independence would mean reabsorption by France. The final settlement of this important question resulted, therefore, in the formation of the new Kingdom of the Netherlands, whereby both Belgium and Holland, united under the same sovereign, would, it was expected, present a sufficiently strong barrier against France. The new kingdom was declared also to be neutral territory. This is the first time that the conception of neutrality was realized with regard to a buffer-state in Western Europe, located between England, France, and Germany. But the conception of neutrality, as applied to the Netherlands, is much older than the Congress of Vienna; and it seems worth while to trace the different schemes dealing with Belgian neutrality before the years 1814–15.[1]

The idea of establishing the neutrality of the Netherlands goes back in history as far as the government of Maria of Hungary, at the time of Emperor Charles V. The former proposed the neutrality of the Belgian provinces on February 8, 1536, in order that they might escape being made the battlefield of Europe during the impending international conflicts. Charles V refused to consider the scheme, as he himself was planning to raise the Netherlands into an independent kingdom, to be governed by the son of Francis I, King of France. This plan, of course, was never carried out.

In 1634 France and Holland concluded a special treaty against Spain, by which the Netherlands should either become an independent kingdom or be divided between the contracting powers. Cardinal Richelieu, the French minister, preferred the idea of an independent Belgium, and went so far as to propose that this kingdom should be permanently neutral. In that way the cornerstone of Spanish power in Europe would have been destroyed. Although neutral, Belgium would have had the right to conclude offensive alliances, but would not enjoy the benefit of having the integrity of its territory guaranteed. If that scheme had been carried out, the Belgians would have had to revolt against Spanish rule. But the Belgians, owing to the presence of strong Spanish armies within their borders, did not revolt. The plan of Richelieu failed. His scheme was, however, taken over by Cardinal Mazarin, minister of Louis XIV. Mazarin had

[1] See R. Dollot, *Les Origines de la neutralité de la Belgique et le système de la Barrière* (1609–1830), Paris, 1902.

first suggested the annexation of Belgium by France, but he met with strong opposition on the part of Holland and England, both interested in keeping the French menace from extending right to their own doors. Changing his mind, Mazarin, in 1658, reverted to Richelieu's plan concerning the creation of an independent and neutral Belgium. This proposal met with the strong opposition of the Dutch "Staatspensionnaris" De Witt, who expressed the fear that such a state would ruin Dutch trade—an independent Belgium would necessarily be given a free Scheldt. He also made it clear that Holland could not forego her right to meddle in the affairs of the Catholic Netherlands, and that the idea of a common protectorate over them would be welcome. Mazarin seems not to have been sincere when proposing his plan. It may be inferred that his main object was to quiet the fear of Holland that the French and the English would use Belgium as a base during their operations against Spain.

When the Treaty of the Barriers (1715) threatened to impose upon Belgium the Dutch garrisons which were maintained for protection against France, the latter presented (February 17) a memoir to Holland, again proposing the status of permanent neutrality for Belgium. The egotism and ill-will of the Dutch defeated this proposal. They would never have consented to the opening of the Scheldt, which was a necessary condition for an independent Belgium. Their policy on this point is made clear by the declaration of the States-General of the United Provinces, when Emperor Joseph II, in 1756, endeavored to obtain the opening of the Scheldt and free shipping on the river. The States-General declared that "the salvation or the loss of the Republic and its inhabitants depended upon this point."

When the Revolution of the Belgians against Austrian rule broke out in 1789, the Elector Frederick-William of Prussia tried in vain to obtain from the other powers, England and Holland, the recognition of the Belgian Republic. He proposed that they should recognize the independence of Belgium and compel the Belgians "to establish a firm, strong constitution, in conformity with the interests of the Allies . . . . ; to create, subject to the advice of the Allies, a respectable military state that would inspire confidence; to avoid alliances with powers, enemies of the Allies, and also trade with them."

As Prussia was ready to make war on Austria, her hereditary enemy, Emperor Leopold II declared that he would, in case of war, cede the "Austrian Netherlands" to France. This England could not have permitted, and therefore that country withdrew support from Prussia, causing the Elector Frederick-William to abandon his plan concerning Belgium.

The French conquest of Belgium entirely changed the policy of the European powers with regard to the Belgian problem. England now saw the French menace facing her own shores, and, according to her traditional policy, began to take measures to avoid the danger. On November 13, 1813, Lord Castlereagh wrote to the English ambassador in Vienna: "I must particularly recommend you to pay attention to Antwerp. . . . . Leaving Antwerp in the hands of France means, or almost means, imposing on us the necessity of a continuous state of war." It was now England that was specially interested in the future status of Belgium, and it is from that country that emanated the idea, forcibly expressed, of establishing a strong bulwark against France by the creation of the neutral kingdom of the Netherlands.   The idea, supported by Prussia, which, as we have seen, had advocated it some years before, was, however, this time expressed by Lord Castlereagh; and the aggrandizement of Holland by its union with Belgium was strongly supported by the Duke of Wellington.   Accordingly, on July 31, 1814, the Belgian provinces were formally handed over to the Prince of Orange, whom the Dutch had made their sovereign the year before.   The arrangement was confirmed by the Congress of Vienna, and made to include Liège and Luxemburg.

The union of Belgium and Holland was the work of diplomacy: the Belgians had not even been consulted. It was an essentially bad combination.   Had the "complete and intimate fusion," of which the diplomats spoke, been possible between both countries, the projectors would have accomplished an admirable work, offering the surest guaranties for the maintenance of European peace and the durability of their own fabric.   But unfortunately the conception was utopian.

Independently of the fact that the Allies disdained to consult the feelings of the Belgian people, they appeared to have lost sight of the moral history of the Netherlands, and to have forgotten those deep-rooted hatreds, jealousies, and dissensions, both religious and political, that had divided the two peoples since the time of their separation in the sixteenth century.   Count Charles Van Hoogendorp, a prominent member of the Dutch chamber, in a pamphlet entitled *Séparation de la Hollande et de la Belgique*, October, 1830 (Amsterdam), himself acknowledged the lack of sympathy between these peoples: "The difference of national character had engendered grievances, and these grievances had excited universal discontent, and national animosity. The division between the two countries existed *de facto*. Instead of a fusion, all the means employed to amalgamate the two people had only served to disunite them still further. This discontent was not the birth of a day; it dates from the first union of the two states."

After peace had been restored in 1815, when Napoleon had suffered defeat at Waterloo, difficulties began at once. In March, 1814, Holland had adopted a constitution. Inspired by the old laws of the United Provinces, it was in the main strongly Protestant. Eleven Dutch, eleven Belgians, and two delegates representing Luxemburg were appointed to transform this constitution into one that could be applied to the new kingdom of the Netherlands. The commission proposed the introduction of equality and toleration for all creeds throughout the kingdom, and the creation of a two-chambered Parliament in which Holland and Belgium were to have an equal number of representatives, although the Belgians had 50 per cent more population. No national capital was specified, but the King was to be invested both at Amsterdam and at some city in Belgium. On these principles a fundamental constitution was drafted and submitted contemporaneously to the Dutch States-General and to the notables of the different Belgian provinces. The Dutch passed it unanimously; the Belgians rejected it by a vote of 1,603 to 527. This rejection was partly due to the unwillingness of the Belgian notables to legalize religious equality. The Dutch King, William I, decided to meet the difficulty in a simple manner.   He announced that all who had abstained from voting should be counted as voting for the act, and that the 126 hostile votes still remaining as a majority against the act after counting in its favor those refraining from voting should not count, as the principle of religious liberty had been imposed by the Congress of Vienna and had to be observed.   This method, which the Belgians called "Dutch arithmetic," gave to the act 933 votes in its favor as against 670 hostile votes, and it was declared passed.

It became more and more clear that William I was not "the right man in the right place": he was too Protestant, too Dutch, too autocratic for the Belgians.   The latter soon complained of new grievances, among which the following were the most important: the imposition of the Dutch language upon all functionaries, whether civil or military, without granting time to learn it to those who could not speak it; the extreme partiality shown in the distribution of all offices and emoluments; and a financial system that bore heavily and unjustly on Belgium.   The Belgians were made to contribute to the payment of debts incurred by Holland long prior to the union, and to pay for the defense of the Dutch colonies, which yielded them no returns at all.   The Haute Cour, or supreme court of justice, and all other great public institutions were established in Holland.   The religious grievances were also numerous: the government was ill disposed toward the Catholics, and it was supposed that it desired to "Protestantize" the people.   Since 1815, the Belgian bishops, under the leadership of Monsignor de Broglie, bishop of Ghent, had dissuaded their flocks from taking the oath to a constitution that introduced liberty of worship. Moreover, in 1825, William I, imitating the plan formerly developed by Joseph II, had established a Philosophic College at Louvain where all priests would receive their education; and, claiming the monopoly for the state in educational matters, had suppressed the episcopal and other national colleges and free schools. Sundry oppressive taxes, repugnant to the habits and usages of the people, were imposed. The freedom of the press was destroyed, and journalists were continually prosecuted before the tribunals. The King even pressed into service ignominious French pamphleteers, expelled from their own country, who daily insulted the Belgians.

This was too much for the descendants of those who had fought the tyrannies of Spain, Austria, and France. Public opinion became excited, and in 1828 a union was concluded between the Catholics, partisans of tradition, and the Liberals, who had adopted the ideas of the French Revolution. Threatened in their common interests and privileges, Catholics and Liberals worked together to obtain redress of their grievances and to defend their liberties.

Like Joseph II, the Dutch King refused to hear their complaints, and continued to offend the Belgian people. In 1830 an event of great importance fanned the revolt into flame.[1] In July the people of Paris overthrew the French legitimist monarchy and the government of Charles X. Just as the Brabant Revolution of 1789 was inspired in the first instance by events in Paris and by the fall of the Bastille, so the "July days" gave the final impulse to the Belgians in August. On the evening of August 25, the Brussels Opera House gave a performance

[1] The history of the establishment of Belgian independence is well described by Ensor, *Belgium*, pp. 123 ff.. whom we largely follow in the narration of the revolution.

of Auber's *La Muette de Portici*.   When the hero of the
piece sang the famous air appealing for revolt and liberty,
the effect on the emotions of his hearers was such as to
cause them to rush into the streets and then and there
inaugurate a revolt against the Dutch.   They sacked the
house of Van Maenen, the unpopular minister of William
I, and that of Libri, the editor of the official governmental
newspaper, and attacked the homes of many against
whom hatred had long been growing.   A guard of citizens
was raised to maintain order and a Committee of Regency
was established in the Hôtel de Ville.   The French tricolor, which had first been hoisted—and this proves the
interference of French clubs at the beginning of the
Revolution—was replaced by the old Brabant tricolor
(black, yellow, red), which is now the Belgian flag.   The
other chief towns followed and confined their Dutch
garrisons within the citadels and forts.   Meanwhile
a deputation was sent to the King, to petition for the
administrative separation of Belgium and Holland,
retaining, however, their personal union.   William I,
unaware of the gravity of the situation, paid scarcely any
attention to the delegates.   He sent a Dutch army nearly
10,000 strong, with many guns, under Prince Frederick,
his younger son, to attack Brussels, where the revolutionists held the lower town.   The troops fought their
way to the very heart of the upper town, but were
stopped at the Place Royale by the stubborn resistance
of the Belgian volunteers.   These were merely Brussels
citizens, reinforced by 300 volunteers from Liège under
Charles Rogier, 200 from Louvain, with Jenneval, author
of the "Brabançonne,"[1] and others from various Walloon

---

[1] As is well known, the "Brabançonne" became the national anthem.

towns.   For three days there was terrible street fighting,
and on the night of September 26–27 Prince Frederick,
with at least 1,500 killed and many wounded, admitted
his defeat and left Brussels.   Meanwhile a provisional
government had been established, composed of Baron
d'Hoogvorst, the commander of the volunteers; Charles
Rogier, who afterward became the Belgian prime minister;
Count Felix de Merode; Van de Weyer, afterward Belgian minister in London; Gendebien, the leader of the
French party among the revolutionists, Joly, and De
Potter.   On October 4, 1830, this provisional government declared Belgium an independent state, and announced its intention of preparing a constitution which
was to be approved and adopted by a national congress.
A special commission decided, on October 12, in favor
of a constitutional monarchy.   The final decree of the
congress establishing this constitution as law was voted
on February 7, 1831.

The basis of the new Belgian constitution consisted
of the charters and privileges of the different Belgian
provinces and cities, which dated from the Middle Ages,
and especially the "Joyeuse Entrée" of Brabant, of which
mention has already been made.   Other liberties, required
by the spirit of modern times, were added: equality of
all the Belgians before the law; freedom of worship, of
the press, of association, of educational teaching, and
the right to vote was accorded to all Belgians who paid
a certain amount in taxes.

Some time after the provisional government had
declared Belgium an independent state a conference of
the powers was held, on November 4, 1830, in London,
to consider the new situation created by the Belgian

revolt: Van der Weyer was sent to represent the Belgian interests. On December 20, a motion made by the British delegate, Lord Palmerston, was adopted, which declared Belgium an "independent power." The victory of the revolutionists was thus confirmed. At the same time, the plan of a small but active party among them, who had attempted the reannexation of the country to France, was defeated.

Another important question was now to be settled— the choice of a monarch for the new kingdom. The Belgian congress excluded the candidacy of the Prince of Orange, who was favored by England and Prussia, since the accession of this prince would mean practically reannexation by Holland. Under the influence of the French sympathizers, led by Gendebien, of the provisional government, and by its president, Surlet de Chokier, the Belgian congress decided to offer the crown to the Duke of Nemours, younger son of the French King, Louis-Philippe. This scheme could not be acceded to by England, since Belgium would then have been under the direct influence of France. The English ministry, on February 4, unanimously resolved to declare war on France if Louis-Philippe accepted the offer. So the French King was compelled to decline it on behalf of his son. Finally, on June 4, 1831, the Belgian congress elected Prince Leopold of Saxe-Cobourg-Gotha, widower of the Princess Charlotte of England. Leopold had fought gallantly in the army of the Allies against Napoleon in 1813 and 1814, and had just refused the crown of Greece. He was solemnly inaugurated at Brussels on June 21 as King of the Belgians. He was considered an English prince, and for the moment France resented his election; but Leopold quieted the jealousy of Louis-Philippe by marrying the daughter of the French King, Louise of Orléans.

Another question to be settled was the delimitation of the boundaries of the new kingdom. On January 20 and 27, the Conference of London had issued two protocols, proposing that Belgium be made a perpetually neutral state; that Holland take all the territory that belonged to the Dutch republic in 1790, and that the Grand Duchy of Luxemburg become an appanage of the house of Orange; that Belgium should be charged with $\frac{16}{31}$ of the national debt of the former United Kingdom of the Netherlands.

These protocols, favorable to Holland, were immediately accepted by the Dutch King, but unequivocally rejected by the Belgians. The second article of the London protocols robbed them of Dutch Flanders—the north of the ancient county—of the towns of Maestricht and Venloo and the strip of Limburg surrounding them, and also of the Grand Duchy, a part of the old Belgian province of Luxemburg. The loss of this territory seemed the more unjust as the inhabitants of those regions had participated in the Belgian revolt and did not desire annexation by Holland.

The negotiations between the powers and the Belgians would never have reached a settlement but for King Leopold. The Belgian King persuaded the Conference of London to supersede its protocols by a declaration in eighteen articles, leaving the matter in dispute to be directly negotiated between Leopold and William of Holland, with the good offices of the great powers. The Dutch King refused to recognize the eighteen articles and, on August 2, twelve days after the accession to the throne of Leopold, invaded Belgium.   King Leopold displayed military skill and courage, but the Belgians had no strong army and their ill-trained troops were badly defeated at Louvain and at Hasselt.   Impending disaster was prevented by the sudden arrival of a French army, sent by Louis-Philippe, to whom the Belgian King had appealed for help.   The French repulsed the Dutch. This intervention of France seriously alarmed the other powers, and especially England.   Fearing that French influence might regain a foothold in the new kingdom, they precipitately drafted another protocol, called the Twenty-four Articles, in place of the former eighteen, and took from Belgium the whole of the area in dispute, except the district of Arlon, in Luxemburg.   Again the Belgians refused to be stripped; but the threat of invasion by a German army finally compelled them to accede.   On November 15, 1831, Belgium, France, and England signed the Treaty of the Twenty-four Articles, to which Russia, Prussia, and Austria soon afterward assented.

This time Holland was unwilling to yield, and the Dutch refused to evacuate the territory they occupied, especially the citadel of Antwerp.   A French army, under Gérard, marched for the second time into Belgium, besieged the Antwerp stronghold, and forced the Dutch to capitulate (1832).   King William continued to refuse to subscribe to any agreement until 1838.   Then, suddenly, he gave his adherence to the Twenty-four Articles. The Conference of London met again and, on April 18, 1839, the final Treaty of London was signed.   The Belgians were given a large reduction in what was agreed should be their contribution to the debt of the Netherlands, but were forced to surrender the territories agreed

upon by the treaty of 1831.   They did it very reluctantly,
but had no other choice.

This Treaty of London is the famous "scrap of paper"
of which the German chancellor spoke so disdainfully on
August 14, 1914.   It settled the external relations of Belgium in Europe.   By that treaty, Belgium was declared to be an independent kingdom and was to remain
"a perpetually neutral state," under the guaranty of the
five great powers.   The neutrality of Belgium had been
imposed upon the new kingdom at the instance chiefly
of England, who desired above all to maintain it as a
bulwark against France.   As King Leopold I himself
writes to Queen Victoria on February 15, 1852, "this
neutrality was in the real interest of this country, but
our good congress here did *not* wish it: it was *imposé*
upon them."

Owing to the fact that so much has been said about
the neutrality of Belgium since the beginning of the present
European war, it seems worth while to explain briefly
what ought to be understood by the words "permanent
neutrality," used by the Conference of London.[1]

Article VII of the Treaty of London declares: "Belgium, within the limits specified in Articles I, II, and IV,
shall form an independent and *perpetually neutral* state.
It shall be bound to observe such neutrality toward all
other states."   A distinction must be made between the
neutrality imposed by this article on Belgium and the
occasional neutrality of a state, which during a war
between other powers wishes to avoid the conflict and,
in a perfectly voluntary manner, proclaims that decision

[1] See Em. Waxweiler, *La Belgique neutre et loyale*, pp. 45 ff., Paris,
Lausanne, 1915; Ch. de Visscher, "The Neutrality of Belgium," *Politica
Quarterly* (1915), pp. 17–40.

to the world.   In the European war of today, the United
States of America is observing such an "occasional"
neutrality.

Permanent neutrality is quite another thing.   History
shows that there are certain countries, certain geographical
zones, which, by virtue of their situation, are in some way
predestined to become periodically the theater of struggles
between nations.   The subjection of such a country to
the exclusive influence of one great power has always
marked a breakdown of the European balance of power.
The idea of placing these zones by means of a treaty in
the position of countries outside the possible zone of
international conflicts corresponds to a general plan of
establishing a régime of peace on the basis of reciprocal
and voluntary restriction of action.   From this point of
view, neutralization is essentially a factor for peace.   It
follows that the state which is perpetually neutral has
not only its own individual meaning and independent
mission, but is an important "wheel" in the general policy.
This is the case with Belgium, as it was established by
the great powers after the revolt of 1830, and that is the
true meaning of the statement that it was to be "perpetually neutral."

Between the neutralized state and the creators of its
neutrality there thus exist reciprocal obligations.   The
contracting powers between them undertake engagements
whereby they guarantee to the neutralized state the
privileged condition of enjoying permanent peace; while
on the other side, the neutralized state accepts the obligations which protect the European balance of power.
In that way, each of the contracting powers is bound not
to attack the neutral state; not to invite it to abandon

its peaceful attitude; to defend it against any power, co-contracting or not, which would compel it to abandon its neutrality. The inviolability of the neutralized territory is agreed upon by this means, for violation would mean for such a state a breach of its own neutrality. On the other hand, the neutralized state must itself defend its neutrality, and adopt all the measures needed for such defense. For this reason, international law holds that a neutralized state which commits an act of defense is not to be considered as being in state of war with the power which violates its neutrality.[1] Moreover, the neutral state must prevent troops or convoys of a belligerent power from passing through its territory.[2] Finally, such a state ought to remain a truly independent state, for if it places or allows itself to be placed in a position of dependence upon another power it destroys the European balance of power, the origin of its international status.

Some authorities on international law[3] maintain that in case of violation of the neutral territory by a belligerent, the contracting powers have not only the right, but the duty, to interfere *ex officio*, and to protect the neutral state by military power, even without the consent of the latter. On this point, however, opinion is divided.

Does the neutral possess the right to conclude alliances with a foreign power? This question is a little more difficult to determine exactly, but it may be settled in the following manner. Every alliance has in view the possibility of an armed conflict. It follows logically from this that the right of the neutral state to contract alliances

[1] Article 10 of the Hague Convention, October 18, 1907.

[2] Article 5 of the Hague Convention.

[3] Despagnée and De Boeck, Descamps, Hagerup, and Blüntschli.

corresponds very closely to its right of making war.   If it is necessary to forbid such a state every alliance which would tend to draw it into an armed conflict with third parties, it ought to be granted without hesitation the right of concluding any understanding which should have for its sole object the protection of the nation against foreign aggression.   And a defensive agreement tending to facilitate for the neutral state the carrying out of the part it is compelled to play in the maintenance of the European balance of power—the very basis of its neutrality—is certainly permissible, and, under certain circumstances, may even seem necessary; for example, when the neutral state seems too weak to resist by its own force a possibly powerful invasion.   But it is obvious that the neutral state may never conclude either an offensive or a defensive alliance which would impose upon it the obligation of possible co-operation in the defense of a foreign territory. That is the true meaning of the permanent neutrality imposed on Belgium by the Treaty of London, and it will become clearer when we look at the subsequent facts of history.

In 1870, on the eve of the Franco-German War, Bismarck, with the object of alienating from France the sympathy of the neutral nations, and especially that of England, published a draft treaty, three or four years old, and in the handwriting of Napoleon III's ambassador, whereby France was to annex Belgium.   This publication aroused public opinion in England, and, giving expression to English feeling, Disraeli told Parliament that "the treaties on which are based the independence and neutrality of Belgium" had been concluded *in the general interest of Europe* and also with a very clear idea of their importance for England. He added: "It is a fundamental principle of the policy of this country, that the country situated along the coasts of Dunkirk to the North Sea islands should be possessed by free and prosperous states practising the arts of peace, in order that these countries should not belong to a great military power." In conformity with these declarations the English government proposed to France and to Prussia to observe the guaranty by way of co-operation between the English forces and the forces of one of the belligerents against the other in case of the violation by the latter of the neutrality of Belgium. This arrangement was accepted on both sides, and laid down in the formal treaties dated August 9 and 11, 1870. Those special treaties were to be in force "during the war and for one year thereafter," and the final paragraph expressly stated that, after this period, the regulations of the Treaty of London (1839) should be regarded as in force.[1] This treaty it was that was thought to protect Belgium when the country's neutrality was violated by Germany on August 3, 1914.

[1] "At the expiration of this term [one year after the War of 1870] the independence and the neutrality of Belgium will continue to be based as before upon Article I of the quintuple Treaty of April 19, 1839."

CHAPTER XIII

INDEPENDENT BELGIUM

In 1832 King Leopold I married Louise-Marie, daughter of the French King Louis-Philippe, who, through her womanly virtues, had made herself greatly beloved. The first Queen of the Belgians died in 1850, leaving three children: Leopold, Duke of Brabant, who afterward became King Leopold II; Philippe, Count of Flanders; and Charlotte, who married Archduke Maximilian of Austria. Under the patronage of Napoleon III, Maximilian was for some years Emperor of Mexico, and 2,000 Belgian volunteers followed him into that country. Napoleon III abandoned him when political troubles broke out in Mexico, and, notwithstanding the stubborn resistance he offered to the army of the Republicans, Maximilian fell into the hands of his enemies and was shot at Queretaro in 1867 by order of Juarez. As a result of this tragedy Empress Charlotte became insane.

Meanwhile the first King of the Belgians had developed the economic resources of Belgium. He was determined in his policy of maintaining the permanent neutrality of the country, as imposed by the Treaty of London. He preserved very friendly relations with Queen Victoria of England, and the correspondence between the two sovereigns shows that the first King of the Belgians would have found in her a mighty protector in the hour of trial. In a letter dated from Buckingham Palace in 1852, Queen Victoria, dealing with the fear of a *coup d'état* on the part of "such an extraordinary man" as Louis-Napoleon—

the future Napoleon III—asserted that any violation of Belgian neutrality would mean a *casus belli* for her government.

How strongly the throne of Leopold I was established among his own people was shown by the fact that during the Revolution of 1848, which nearly resulted in the overthrow of all the thrones of Europe, Belgium alone kept herself aloof from the European turmoil, and some French adventurers who had tried to cross the frontier and, with the help of some unpatriotic Belgians, to proclaim a republic on Belgian soil, were quickly disarmed in the skirmish at Risquons-Tout, near Mouscron, in West Flanders. King Leopold consistently regarded himself as a constitutional king, and won thereby the confidence and the respect of the nation. During his reign Belgium gave many proofs of her spirit of enterprise and economic vitality. In 1835 she constructed the first railway that existed on the Continent, connecting Brussels and Malines. The country likewise prepared itself for defense against foreign invasion, and built the fortifications of Antwerp, making this city the ultimate bulwark of national defense. In 1860, the octrois, a sort of communal customs levied upon entering Belgian towns, were abolished; and in 1863 the tolls of the Scheldt, paid to the Dutch by all vessels coming from Antwerp, were discontinued.

From a political point of view the old union of 1828 between Catholics and Liberals had disappeared. From 1847 the personnel of the ministries was no longer composed of members of both parties, but of representatives of one party only, to the exclusion of those of the other. The Liberals were in power from 1847 to 1855; the Catholics followed, and they in turn retired before a street riot in

1857; the Liberals again held power throughout the reign of Leopold I. The first King of the Belgians died on December 10, 1865.

The Duke of Brabant succeeded him under the name of Leopold II. Born on April 9, 1835, in 1853 he married Marie-Henriette, Archduchess of Austria, who died in 1902. The only son of this marriage, the Count of Hainaut, died at the age of ten years, in 1869.

During the reign of Leopold II, both Catholics and Liberals came, in turn, into power, the Liberals from 1857 to 1870; the Catholics from 1870 to 1878; the Liberals again until 1884. Since that time a Catholic ministry has ruled the destinies of the nation. For the first time the Socialist party gained a foothold in Parliament through the elections of 1894.

The material conditions of Belgium—its trade and industry—enjoyed unusual development under Leopold II. This sovereign endeavored to place Belgian capital in large industrial and commercial enterprises all over the world, and it was during his reign that the Belgians obtained recognition and influence in China, South America, and Persia. His solicitude for the welfare of Antwerp is well known, as well as his strong policy in favor of the development of the military organization of Belgium. The forts on the Meuse were his work, and the characteristic remark which he made when taunting a member of the Belgian Parliament for opposing the contemplated fortification is well known: "Never go out without an umbrella, Sir!" The reform and the increase of the Belgian army was also largely due to Leopold II; and the importance he attached to this matter made him very unpopular in many quarters, where opposition existed to what was termed "militarism." His reign cannot yet strictly be said to belong to history, as he died in December, 1910. In 1885, by the Congress of Berlin, the European powers had recognized the Congo as an independent state under the sovereignty of the Belgian King. After his death it became, by a vote of the Belgian Parliament, a national colony.

And the present King of the Belgians, His Majesty Albert I, is now the young hero for whom all the countries of the world, except perhaps those whose rulers are his enemies, have, since the beginning of the European war, come to entertain a lively admiration and respect. He is well termed "the knight without fear and without reproach."

EPILOGUE

At the present writing Belgium is involved in the fearful struggle that has set the world aflame. In respect to Belgium, many facts of this war have already been placed beyond dispute as much as any fact of history can be.[1] Nevertheless, it is not our task to deal with her heroic resistance to the violation of her neutrality, her sufferings, and her sorrows. These are not yet history. But, whatever may be the result of the war which the country is now waging for liberty, let us at least remember two facts which will shed light on the future. The first is that England, now supported by France, Russia, and Italy, undoubtedly recalls the words spoken by Disraeli in 1870, asserting—to quote them once more—that "it is a fundamental principle of the policy of this country that the country situated along the coasts of Dunkirk to the North Sea islands should be possessed by free and prosperous states . . . . in order that these countries should not belong to a great military power."

The second fact is, that he who is acquainted with the history of Belgium through the ages—the unflinching character of its people, and the love for liberty and independence which successively inspired the victors of the battle of the Golden Spurs, the six hundred Franchimontois who gave their lives to save Liège from the outrage of Charles the Bold, duke of Burgundy, the revolt against Spain, the Brabant Revolution of 1789, the War of the Peasants against the "Sans-culottes," and the citizens who fought Prince Frederick of Holland in the streets of Brussels—can reach but one conclusion: Belgians never will be slaves!

[1] See on the "case of Belgium" in the European war the book by J. M. Beck, *The Evidence in the Case*, New York, 1915, 2d ed.

167

BIBLIOGRAPHY

The best work to be consulted on the history of Belgium is that by H. Pirenne, professor in the University of Ghent, entitled *Histoire de Belgique*, Vols. I–IV, Brussels, 1900–1911. The work is not yet complete: the fourth volume carries us down to 1648. Those wishing to study more in detail the various problems of Belgian history will find the enumeration of original sources and modern books in H. Pirenne, *Bibliographie de l'histoire de Belgiques*, 2d ed., Brussels, 1902. For a list of books published since 1902 see the Belgian periodical *Archives belges*, where the important books and articles on Belgian history are reviewed and discussed.

Works written in English are the following: Demetrius C. Boulger, *A History of Belgium*, 2 vols., London, 1902–9; J. de C. MacDonnell, *Belgium, Her Kings, Kingdom and People*, London, 1914; R. C. K. Ensor, *Belgium*, New York and London [1915]. The work by Boulger is mainly based on the old work of Théodore Juste, *Histoire de Belgique* (new edition in 3 vols., Brussels, 1895), which is not up to date and cannot be compared with Pirenne's *Histoire*. The works by MacDonnell and Ensor deal especially with the contemporary history of Belgium, the former treating Belgian politics from the Catholic point of view, the latter being frequently ill informed and unjust toward the Catholic party. Both have their merits in dealing with the history of Belgium in the nineteenth century. Modern Belgium has also been studied by H. Charriaut, *la Belgique moderne*, Paris, 1910. This book offers much information, but contains many misstatements. For social problems, see B. Seebohm Rowntree, *Land and Labour: Lessons from Belgium*, London, 1910. In French there exists an excellent survey of the most important periods of Belgian history, written by G. Kurth, *la nationalité belge*, Brussels, 1913.

A very readable book, well written and well illustrated, based on accurate historical information, and dealing with the history of Flanders in the largest sense of the word, is the work of Edward Neville Vose, *The Spell of Flanders*, Boston, Page Co., 1915. The author, describing the visit he made to various Flemish towns, gives a good account of the most striking facts of their history.